Autism, Ethnicity and Culture

PORTLAND
PUBLIC LIBRARY

ENRICHING OUR COMMUNITY,
EXPANDING OUR WORLD.

of related interest

A Guide to Mental Health Issues in Girls and
Young Women on the Autism Spectrum
Diagnosis, Intervention and Family Support
Dr Judy Eaton
ISBN 978 1 78592 092 9
eISBN 978 1 78450 355 0

Drinking, Drug Use, and Addiction in the Autism Community
Elizabeth Kunreuther and Ann Palmer
Foreword by Tony Attwood
ISBN 978 1 78592 749 2
eISBN 978 1 78450 539 4

Re-Thinking Autism
Diagnosis, Identity and Equality
Edited by Katherine Runswick-Cole, Rebecca Mallett and Sami Timimi
ISBN 978 1 84905 581 9
eISBN 978 1 78450 027 6

AUTISM, ETHNICITY AND CULTURE

Working with Children and Families from Minority Communities

DR PRITHVI PEREPA

Foreword by Professor Rita Jordan

Jessica Kingsley *Publishers*
London and Philadelphia

First published in 2019
by Jessica Kingsley Publishers
73 Collier Street
London N1 9BE, UK
and
400 Market Street, Suite 400
Philadelphia, PA 19106, USA

www.jkp.com

Library of Congress Cataloging in Publication Data
Names: Perepa, Prithvi, author.
Title: Autism, ethnicity and culture : working with children and families
    from minority communities / Prithvi Perepa ; foreword by Professor Rita
    Jordan.
Description: London ; Philadelphia : Jessica Kingsley Publishers, 2019.
Identifiers: LCCN 2018035667 | ISBN 9781785923609
Subjects: LCSH: Autistic children--Services for. | Parents of autistic
    children--Services for. | Social work with minorities. | Social work with
    children with disabilities.
Classification: LCC RJ506.A9 P474 2019 | DDC 618.92/85882--
dc23 LC record available at https://lccn.loc.gov/2018035667

British Library Cataloguing in Publication Data
A CIP catalogue record for this book is available from the British Library

ISBN 978 1 78592 360 9
eISBN 978 1 78450 701 5

Printed and bound in Great Britain

Contents

Foreword

The first thought that occurs when reading this book is to wonder why this is the first serious attempt to get to grips with this topic when it is clearly so important for our understanding of autism and our attempts to provide effective education and support. I knew of Dr Perepa's work in this area, since I had the privilege of supervising his PhD, but I had assumed that my lack of more recent knowledge was because I had lost touch; this excellent review of the topic shows how rudimentary our knowledge still is, and how much we still need to learn.

This book is more than an academic review of the literature; the author's background as a practitioner and his wide experience in education and support mean he is well able to draw out and discuss the implications of the research. In particular, while being academically rigorous, this book is directed at practitioners of all kinds and includes 'pauses' at the end of each chapter where practitioners are encouraged to reflect on what they have read and relate it to their own practice.

I hope this book will have the influence it deserves to have. It could be an excellent springboard for further research, which is much needed. Perhaps, more importantly, it brings ethnicity to the attention of those trying to develop person-centred practice and gives practical guidance on the issues that need to be addressed. It shows that there are no simplistic answers, while being an important first step in helping us understand how ethnicity may affect not only the behaviour of those with autism, but also the interpretation that parents and professionals place on that behaviour. It deserves a wide readership, and this will be helped by its clear, direct style.

Professor Rita Jordan BSc, MSc, MA, PhD, CPsych, OBE

Acknowledgements

I would like to thank Andrew James from Jessica Kingsley Publishers for approaching me with the idea for this book. Although autism and ethnicity has been the focus of a lot of my work over the last 20 years I had not considered writing a book on this topic, and without Andrew this may not have happened. Thanks also to my colleague Marie Howley who provided constructive feedback on the first two chapters. Finally, thanks to my family who continuously checked my progress and encouraged me to keep writing, especially to Colin for challenging some of my ideas and ensuring that what I wrote was clear.

Chapter 1

AUTISM AND
—— ETHNICITY ——

Autism is considered to be a developmental disability that impacts the individual's ability to communicate and interact with others. It also affects their ability to think flexibly, which can be exhibited via adherence to routines, rituals and difficulty in coping with change. Some people with autism may also have different sensory perceptions (APA 2013). Current prevalence rates of the condition in the UK are estimated to be around 1 in 100 (Baird *et al.* 2006; Baron-Cohen *et al.* 2009), and in the USA it is as high as 1 in 68 (Baio *et al.* 2018). This makes it a very common condition that professionals from various backgrounds, such as health, social care and education, will come across. One of the difficulties with autism is that although it is agreed that the above-mentioned areas are affected in everyone who has a diagnosis of autism, there is a difference in the levels to which these impact each individual. Hence, in the literature and in professional circles, the term 'spectrum' is used, as in autism spectrum disorders (ASD) or autism spectrum conditions (ASC). There have been attempts to sub-categorise autism based on the severity of the condition into labels such as severe autism, high-functioning autism, Asperger syndrome and atypical autism. There is increasing scepticism about the relevance and accuracy of these different labels, which is reflected in the latest version of the *Diagnostic and Statistical Manual of Mental Disorders*, 5th edition (DSM-5), produced by the American Psychiatric Association (APA) (2013), where it was decided to use the term 'autism spectrum disorder' as the only term to define all individuals with the condition.

The term 'disorder' is divisive within the field, with some stating that autism is a difference and does not necessarily disable people, whereas others argue that while this might be true for some individuals on the spectrum, it can be disabling for others. This perhaps reflects the impact of the diversity of symptoms that are collated under this label. Although discussion around vocabulary and labelling is topical, this is not the main focus of this book, and so I am not going to explore them any further here. However, I have decided to use the terms 'autism', 'autism spectrum' or 'spectrum' to represent all manifestations of the condition in this book. Similarly, some adults with autism prefer identity-first language, and use 'autistic person' rather than 'person with autism'. Again, this view is not shared by all people with or without autism across various parts of the world. Therefore, I am using a person-first language format of 'individual with autism' throughout the book, as the intention is to consider the whole breadth of the spectrum.

Why autism and ethnicity?

Our identity is described using words such as 'race', 'ethnicity' and 'culture'. These are often used as synonyms.

Before we proceed any further, we discuss these terms here in order to make clear the similarities and differences between them.

'Race' is a term that was initially popularised by biologists with the view that humans could be separated into different groups based on their skin colour and features. It was assumed that these differences were genetically based. This view is mostly discredited now, as people from so-called different races are often genetically close to each other. 'Ethnicity' is a preferred term by anthropologists who use this to mean a group of people who have shared ancestry, heritage, culture and customs. However, most people in the West use ethnicity as a different word for country or continent of origin, such as British Pakistani or Korean American. 'Culture' can be defined as the distinctive way of life of a group, based on similar values (including childrearing and social relationships), language and/or religion (O'Hagan 2001), which are learned, shared and transmitted from one generation to another (Mink 1997). Of course not all cultural values have similar importance to people within a given family. These may be based on other factors such as gender, sexual orientation or disability. Children learn about their culture from a variety of sources: through routine exchanges and relationships between family members and families, literature and media, through contacts with peers, and often through the differentiation of 'insiders' from 'outsiders' (Ahmad *et al.* 1998). I use ethnicity and culture as synonyms in this book, especially as much published data often use these terms as such.

Although it is assumed that autism affects everyone at the same rate across all ethnicities (Fombonne 2007), our understanding of autism in various ethnic communities is limited. We have only recently started looking at this in any detail. This is surprising since many Western countries have been multicultural for decades, and cultural factors have been the focus of attention in the area of mental health and psychiatry for a longer period. Commenting about the lack of interest regarding culture and autism among professionals in the field across the world, Cuccaro *et al.* (1996) suggest three possible reasons for this:

- A residual effect of early descriptions that autism is more common in upper socio-economic status (SES) White families.

- A focus on the neuro-biological basis of autism, which does not give importance to the study of variables such as culture.

- The apparent lack of differences among various cultures in the expression, incidence and prevalence of autism.

Although none of the above statements has been proven, it is possible that these views of autism held within the field could be partly responsible for the lack of research in the subject until recently. Knowledge and understanding of these issues has since changed, and there is more interest in this topic, as can be seen from a dedicated book on the subject, but this remains a minority interest in the field of autism.

This lack of information and interest is not just limited to professionals working in the field, but also parents from minority ethnic communities who have a child with autism are often not aware of anyone else from their community who has this condition. I realised this when I was conducting research for my doctoral study and trying to involve parents from various ethnic backgrounds. Since I was finding it hard to recruit parents from minority ethnic communities living in London, I thought that I would request parents to refer someone else they knew in their community whose family was affected by autism. Most were unable to help me with this, as they did not know of anyone thus affected from their community. This was not the case with participants from a White British background who were often involved in networks and were able to signpost me to others with a family member with autism. I started wondering why this difference in experience exists if autism is as common across cultures, as suggested in the research. This question guided part of my doctoral study and provides an impetus for this book that explores the role of ethnicity in the field of autism, and I hope that this will inform development and access to better services. In this book I intend to explore the way autism is conceptualised, the issues with diagnostic procedures and practices, as well as wider issues in accessing services for families from minority ethnic communities.

Conceptualisation of autism

Before focusing on the role of ethnicity in understanding autism, it is useful to identify the accepted medical version of autism and its historical roots, because this was the view that conceptualised autism as a discrete condition and that came up with characteristics which separate it from other disabilities. Having this knowledge as a basis will help in understanding where, and if, culture and ethnicity influence how we conceptualise autism, and provide support for individuals coming from different ethnic backgrounds.

Before the label of 'autism' was coined, children with autism would have been treated in a variety of ways based on the social norms at the time. There are stories of 'changelings whose souls were taken' and a variety of other folktales and myths in popular culture in the West. French physician Jean-Marc-Gaspard Itard, who is often considered the father of special education, was one of the first people to maintain detailed notes of a boy called Victor who was found in the woods of Aveyron in central France, and he published this work in 1801 (translated by Lane 1977). If the concept of autism existed at that time, Victor would have been diagnosed with the condition; in the absence of such a term, Victor was called other names. Medicalisation of childhood behaviour had not yet taken place.

It was in 1867 that Henry Maudsley suggested that children who showed unusual behaviours were perhaps experiencing childhood psychosis. Once the concept of childhood psychosis was accepted, a number of professionals wrote case studies of children whose behaviours were unusual. Unfortunately not all of these were detailed enough to provide an in-depth understanding of the conditions. It was in this era that Leo Kanner (1943) and Hans Asperger (1944; see Frith 1991) wrote their own case studies of children they considered to be unusual. Kanner worked with 11 children and considered that they displayed behaviours that were unlike any other childhood disorder known at that time. Asperger worked with over 200 children and reported four case studies in his work published in 1944. Both these men are acknowledged as having identified autism as a distinct condition from intellectual disabilities or mental health conditions. In his initial work Kanner (1943) suggested the key features of autism as:

- An extreme 'autistic aloneness'

- Excellent rote memory

- Mutism or unusual language development

- Unusual responses to sensory stimuli

- Obsessive desire for maintaining sameness

- Good relationship with objects but not with people

- Good cognitive potential.

Unlike Kanner, Asperger did not specify the characteristics he considered as essential for autism in his paper from 1944. However, from his descriptions, the following characteristics can be identified as features that drew his attention to these children:

- Aristocratic appearance

- Limited facial and gestural expressions, and peculiar eye gaze

- Unusual intonation and pitch

- Capability to produce original ideas but may not follow others

- Specialised interests and obsessions

- Ability to engage in introspection and focused on bodily functions

- Disturbance in forming relationships with their environment and people

- Could have a wide range of cognitive abilities

- Engages in stereotypical activities and self-stimulatory behaviours

- Over- or under-sensitivity to stimulation

- Extremely egocentric

- Motor clumsiness

- Unusual relationship with objects and abnormal fixations

- Lack of a sense of humour.

Both Asperger and Kanner believed that autism was more common in highly educated and intelligent families, or that it was a middle-class condition. Although attempts were made by the Dutch professional, van Krevelen (1971), to publicise Asperger's work, it did not draw attention in the English-speaking world until the late 1980s. Until that happened, the concept of autism was being developed based on Kanner's case studies. The term 'autism' itself was still not a universally accepted term, and there was often confusion between autism and schizophrenia. Attempts were being made to come up with a way to capture these differences, and in 1964 Creak published a report from the working committee she was chairing, which suggested nine potential points found in these children. However, these were not objective enough to be used as diagnostic criteria, and some argued that there was still an overlap between autism and schizophrenia. A number of other similar attempts were made by various professionals to capture the features that make autism unique.

In 1971 Rutter, Bartak and Newman suggested that children would need to meet the following four criteria to be identified with autism:

- Delay in speech and language development

- An autistic-like failure to develop interpersonal relationships

- Ritualistic and compulsive phenomena

- Onset before 30 months.

Rutter (1978) later expanded these criteria and provided examples of 'autistic-like failure'. These included:

- Lack of eye gaze

- Failure to become attached to parents, including not seeking comfort from others

- Little or no separation anxiety

- Apparent lack of interest in people

- Little variation in facial expressions

- Lack of preference for familiar adults

- Failure to make friends and to join in with group activities.

Rutter's conceptualisation of the condition influenced the criteria used in the third version of the *Diagnostic and Statistical Manual of Mental Disorders* (DSM-III, APA 1980), which, for the first time, defined infantile autism with separate diagnostic criteria from childhood schizophrenia. It took 40 years before the concept of autism was agreed and criteria were developed to identify this condition, mainly by professionals from the UK and the USA. Even so, the new criteria were not necessarily applicable for people of all ages. As can be seen from the name, it was considered to be a childhood condition, and the new diagnostic criteria were, as such, applicable to younger children rather than individuals across the age range.

Around the same time, Wing and Gould (1979) undertook an epidemiological study and suggested the 'triad of impairments' of (a) social interaction, (b) language and communication and (c) thought and behaviour as the core features of autism. Their criteria did not necessarily include all the features defined by Kanner and broadened the criteria significantly from its original beginnings, thereby introducing the idea of an autistic continuum. The revised third version of the DSM, DSM-III-R (APA 1987), was based on criteria suggested by Wing and Gould, and the earlier concept of the condition became more fluid. The terminology changed from 'infantile autism' to 'autistic disorder', and it was no longer necessary for features of autism to develop before 30 months of age. This broadened the applicability of the diagnostic criteria to individuals across the age range.

Since then, the key characteristics have been revised many times over the years, both in the DSM and the International Classification of Diseases (ICD), which is published by the World Health Organization (WHO). The following section briefly goes through some of the characteristics associated with autism at present. Although I define four areas, it should be noted that the latest version of the DSM has only two main areas: social communication and interaction, and repetitive, rigid and ritualistic behaviours. I have divided these into four areas for ease of understanding. I begin with explaining the features of autism because familiarity with these and some of the cognitive theories that are used to explain the behaviours found in autism is important for understanding how cultural perceptions could have been influential in developing the criteria and cognitive theories.

Key characteristics associated with autism
Social communication

People with autism are considered to have unusual language and communication skills. This could mean that some people may never develop any speech, while others may have speech, but this does not always lead to good communication skills. In fact, autism is one of the few conditions where structural aspects of language (such as vocabulary and grammar) can develop without necessarily understanding the subtleties of language. In regressive autism, children could develop speech and communication skills and then lose this at a later stage, usually around the ages of two to three. Other possible differences include echolalia or repetitive speech, and semantic and pragmatic difficulties, for example, with pronouns, literal understanding and issues in following the norms of communication. Taking language at its face value could make it difficult to understand jokes, sarcasm and idioms. Some individuals with autism find it difficult to communicate for social purposes other than meeting their needs. Others can also find understanding and using non-verbal aspects of communication (such as intonation, gestures and facial expressions) difficult. A substantial proportion of human communication is dependent on non-verbal means. Without understanding these signs it can be difficult to interpret when it is our turn to speak or what our communication partner is feeling. It is no wonder, then, that individuals with autism, even with sophisticated language skills, may find communication a challenge.

Social interaction

Difficulties and differences in social interaction are often considered to be the most obvious characteristic of autism. Differences in social interaction range from individuals who appear as if they do not want to interact with others, to those who would like to interact but who make social mistakes. Some will find it easier to interact with older or younger people rather than their peers. Others will interact only with familiar people and when the interaction is initiated by someone else. These difficulties with interaction are not limited to childhood and later years; in fact, some of the autism screening tools have identified the following as potential signals of autism in children as young as 18 months:

- Unusual eye contact

- Not engaging in joint attention or spontaneous sharing of interests

- Limited or unusual expression of emotions.

Adults with autism often state that they find it difficult to understand unwritten social rules, which can in some cases lead to anxiety about social interaction. These differences in social understanding can also lead to unusual emotional responses. Baron-Cohen, Leslie and Frith (1985) argue that people with autism lack theory of mind, our ability to understand that other people have different thoughts, feelings and knowledge from our own. According to Baron-Cohen *et al.* (1985), this could be the reason why individuals with autism find social interactions difficult, as they are unable to understand or predict other people's behaviour.

Flexible thinking

The terms 'repetitive', 'rigid' and 'ritualistic' behaviours are sometimes used to explain this area, as mentioned above. Individuals with autism may find it difficult to deal with change, and may insist on keepings things familiar. Some will also engage in stereotypical and repetitive body movements, such as rocking or flicking fingers. Repetitive speech patterns such as asking the same question over and over are also noticed in some. Two theories attempt to explain these differences. The first is the executive functioning difficulties theory. According to Ozonoff (1995), this can make it difficult for a person with autism to plan and monitor their actions, shift their attention from one task to another, hold relevant information in their working memory and inhibit their impulses. Because of this, someone with autism could insist on doing the same activities over and over again, and when disturbed may have to start from the beginning. Lawson, Baron-Cohen and Wheelwright (2004) suggest an alternative empathising and systemising theory. According to them, while individuals with autism may find it difficult to empathise with others (poor empathisers), they are good at finding patterns and constructing systems (good systemisers). According to this theory, systemising means that the individual likes to keep the system they have developed the same; hence ritualistic and rigid behaviours occur.

Other behaviours that can be seen under this area include children with autism who may find it difficult to engage in pretend play with other children but who perhaps engage in imaginative play on their own. Frith (1989), in her weak central coherence theory, argues that one of the main differences in autism is that people with the condition find it harder to understand the overall gist of a situation and tend to focus on the details. This, of course, may make it difficult for an individual to generalise what is learned in one situation to another or to see the relevance of what is being learned in the long term. This could especially be an issue when what is being taught is not part of the few special interests the individual may have.

Sensory differences

Although both Kanner and Asperger identified unusual sensory responses in their case studies in their seminal pieces of work, this area seems to have been lost in the later criteria of autism developed by other academics in the field. Only recently has there been more focus on this area again. It has been suggested that some individuals with autism could have an over- or under-reaction to their environment (APA 2013). This could then lead to the person finding daily sensory stimulations such as someone talking or touching them unbearable. Or on the other hand, those who are under-reactive to sensations may make extra efforts to seek the sensation they need, at the intensity they want. Sensory perception differences occur because the brain is unable to interpret information received from the different senses and to organise its reactions accordingly (Ayers 1979).

Although sensory perception differences can be observed in people without autism, Leekam *et al.* (2007) argue that these are more common and persistent in individuals on the spectrum. Some suggest that behaviour patterns commonly associated with autism, such as rocking, flapping or closing their ears, could all have a sensory basis, and that the individual is engaged in such behaviour to self-regulate.

Is the prevalence of autism the same in all ethnicities?

Until recently most of the autism-related literature assumed that the prevalence of autism would be the same across ethnicities and countries of the world. Although there were some studies in the past that raised doubts about this, over the past decade or so there is growing evidence to suggest that this assumption might be naïve. As can be seen from the figures at the beginning of this chapter, there are even differences between English-speaking countries such as the UK and the USA. The difficulty with finding accurate prevalence rates for autism is that not many countries actually collect this data. Where such data are collected, they tend to focus on school-age children rather than across the lifespan. Therefore, many of the reported figures are estimates rather than concrete figures.

When they are available, prevalence rates of autism across the world vary significantly. If we continue looking at the figures in the Western world, Sotgiu *et al.* (2011) report that in the Piedmont region of Italy the rate of prevalence is 1.7 cases per 1000 in children under the age of 18 (Regione Piemonte, 2008, cited by Sotgiu *et al.* 2011). Based on their recent study completed in Germany, Bachmann, Gerste and Hoffmann (2018) suggest that the prevalence rate among children aged 6–11 years is 0.38 per cent, much below that of other European countries like Italy or the UK.

Moving away from the Western world, Kim *et al.* (2011) conducted one of the first epidemiological studies of autism in school-aged children in South Korea. Their study included all children in the country between the ages of 7 and 12. Based on this, they estimate that the prevalence rate of autism is 2.64 per cent. This is, in fact, one of the highest rates of autism prevalence in the world.

On the other hand, the prevalence rate of autism in Havana in Cuba for children aged 3–13 is reported as 0.4 per 1000 children (various authors, 2003, cited by Sotgiu *et al.* 2011), probably one of the lowest rates. On the basis of their research conducted in 2009 on the prevalence of autism in Oman, Al-Farsi *et al.* (2011) suggest a prevalence rate of 1.4 per 10,000 in children under the age of 14.

The figures are not only different between countries but also among the various studies conducted in the same country. For example, in their systematic literature review of prevalence rates of autism in China, where Wan *et al.* (2013) reviewed 24 published studies that looked at autism in children under the age of 18, they found that figures ranged from 1.8 to 424.6 per 10,000. Of course, it could be argued that low figures of prevalence are a reflection of the lack of awareness of autism in some countries, lack of access to appropriate services, assessment tools used, age of diagnosis, and, in fact, even environmental factors that can vary from country to country. The next section briefly looks at how figures differ based on ethnicity in Europe and the USA.

Prevalence rates of minority ethnic communities

Most of the research that has focused on ethnic disparity in the diagnosis of autism has emerged from the USA and the UK. A few studies conducted in Europe (e.g., El Bouk *et al.* 2009) have reported that compared to White children, children from minority ethnic communities are less likely to receive a diagnosis of autism. The picture in the USA is a little more mixed. Dyches *et al.* (2004) argue that the prevalence rates vary even among children from minority ethnic communities. Citing reports from the US Department of Education (2001, 2002) as evidence, Dyches *et al.* (2004) suggest that children coming from Black or Asian/Pacific Island backgrounds are twice as likely to be classified as having autism compared to children identified as being American Indian or Hispanic. More recent studies such as those by Liptak *et al.* (2008) and Mandell *et al.* (2009) suggest that children from minority ethnic communities are less likely to receive a diagnosis of autism compared to children from a White American background. Similar views are also shared in a report produced by the Centers for Disease Control and Prevention (CDC) (2014). This shows that while the overall rate of autism prevalence is estimated at 14.7 per 1000, the rate among White American children is 15.8 per 1000 whereas the prevalence rates among African American and Latino children are at 12.3 and 10.8 per 1000 respectively.

In the UK there are currently no studies looking at the overall prevalence rates of autism based on ethnicity, as far as I am aware. Lindsay, Pather and Strand (2006) looked at the identified primary need of children who have a statement of special educational needs (SEN) in schools in the UK and identified that, as in the USA, not all groups from minority ethnic groups necessarily follow the figures suggested for autism in the country. However, children from a South Asian background are less likely, compared to White British children, to receive a statement of SEN for autism. Similarly, Marchant, Hussain and Hall (2006) conducted a study where they gathered data from 13 local education authorities (LEAs) to investigate if there was any difference in the percentage of children from different ethnic backgrounds receiving a statement of SEN for autism. They, too, found that compared to White British children, children from a South Asian background are three times less likely to receive a statement of SEN for autism. It should be highlighted here that a statement of SEN is not a diagnosis, but rather an educational provision document (similar to the Individuals with Disabilities Education Act in the USA), which suggests the kind of support that a child will need within an educational setting.

One of the focuses for epidemiological studies has been to see if there is a difference in children identified as being on the autism spectrum based on immigration history. Initial studies conducted in the UK (Wing 1980) and Sweden (Gillberg et al. 1987) have suggested that children born to non-European immigrant parents are more likely to be diagnosed with autism compared to native children. As a result, Gillberg, Steffenberg and Schaumann (1991) have suggested that the increase in the prevalence of autism could partly be explained by the increase in immigrant communities in Europe. This view seems to have been confirmed by subsequent studies such as the one conducted by Goodman and Richards (1995), that found that autism was four to six times more likely in children born to African Caribbean parents compared to White British children. High rates of autism in immigrants who are not from Europe or North America have been reported in a number of other studies in countries such as Denmark and Sweden (Kolevzon, Gross and Reichenberg 2007). Barnevik-Olsson, Gillberg and Fernell (2008) have reported that children from Somalian immigrant families living in Sweden had three to four times more likelihood of being diagnosed with autism compared to Swedish children. Williams et al. (2008) made a similar conclusion from their study, and suggested that children born to parents from North East or South East Asia are at a high risk of being identified with autism.

As is evident from the above discussion, most of these studies tend to focus on non-European immigrants. One of the few studies that does not do this was conducted by Harper and Williams in 1976, who suggested that children born to parents who had emigrated from Greece or Germany to Australia were more likely to be diagnosed with infantile autism. A more recent study that attempted to do this was conducted by Keen, Reid and Arnone (2010), who compared the likelihood of autism in children born to mothers who were born in the UK compared to those who were born outside the UK (including Europe). They also explored if there were any differences based on the place of habitation within the host country by comparing families living in two parts of London. They concluded that irrespective of the social economic status of the local area, children born to mothers from Africa, the Caribbean and Asia had an increased risk of being diagnosed with autism compared to UK-born mothers. Within these three groups, it was children of a mother born in the Caribbean Islands who had the highest risk, with the estimated likelihood being five times compared to children of UK-born mothers. They report that similar differences were not seen in children born to European mothers.

Immigration status seems to have drawn less interest in the USA where far fewer studies have been conducted on this aspect, although studies have been undertaken by Croen, Grether and Selvin (2002) and Schieve et al. (2012). Both studies concluded that children of foreign-born Latino parents were less likely to be identified with autism compared to those of US-born parents. These studies are unusual compared to the others reported above, where immigration status has always been associated with an increased likelihood of autism.

Based on the professional background and training of the researchers, a variety of possible suggestions has been made to explain this difference in prevalence rates among minority ethnic communities in the Western world. These range from biochemical differences, such as lack of vitamin D and change in diet, to sociological factors, such as lack of awareness among these communities, and professionals lacking the skills to diagnose autism in children born from minority ethnic communities. Some of these are explored further in the following chapters of this book.

As can be seen from the above discussion there is little agreement that the prevalence rates of autism are the same across different ethnicities. There would appear to be cases of both over- and under-representation based on ethnicity, or in some instances, people from the same ethnicity were considered to be both over- and under-diagnosed based on different studies. This highlights that there are wide differences in prevalence figures of autism in different countries as well as among different ethnicities living in the same country.

A point I would like to raise here is about the conceptualisation of autism and the potential impact of this on the prevalence figures across the world, but also among different ethnic groups living in the West. As can be seen from the above discussion on the conceptualisation of autism, this was mainly undertaken by professionals from the West, and especially from the UK and the USA. It was then assumed that this so-formed condition would be the same across the world in different ethnic and cultural groups. So why was it assumed that this concept would be universal? Owusu-Bempah and Howitt (2000) feel that the field of psychology imposes Western European and North American values on the whole world. They term this as a form of 'cultural imperialism', and argue that as a result, the field of psychology perpetuates the idea that Western values are right and natural. Taking a similar view, Berry and Kim (1993) criticise the field of psychology as being culturally blind and culturally bound. They say that the field does not acknowledge that its own development is in a specific cultural setting, and that many of its theories and findings may not be applicable to other cultures. It was perhaps this that led professionals working in the field of autism in the West to assume that autism is a universally agreed condition.

Absolutism, relativism and universalism

This section further explores the comments made above about the culturally bound nature of psychology. Berry (1999) and Berry et al. (1999) identified three different stances that can be taken when looking at psychological theories and concepts from a cross-cultural perspective: absolutism, relativism and universalism. According to Berry (1999), absolutists believe that all human phenomena are the same across different cultures. Because culture is viewed as having little relevance in the way humans behave, according to this stance, adopting concepts and standardising measures across different cultures would not cause any problems. Explaining the reason for this lack of attention to cultural influence, Berry et al. (1999) say that this is due to absolutists' belief that behaviour is influenced mainly by biological factors. Absolutists take the view that psychologically people are very similar, and that where differences occur, they are only quantitative in nature – for example, people are just 'less intelligent' or 'more depressed'. Researchers taking this position ignore that their own knowledge is influenced by their cultural context and how it views phenomena. Absolutists do not consider that there is any problem in making comparisons and do so on a frequent basis, as they presume that the phenomena will have the same psychological meaning in most cultures. Berry *et al.* (1999) argue that since these instruments are likely to be biased procedurally as well as conceptually, an absolutist position leads to an imposed etic position. This means that the concepts or theories are developed by people outside the social group where it is being used. I feel that this is the position that most research in the field of autism takes, where the concept and indicators of the condition are considered to be the same everywhere. Therefore, the conceptualisation of the condition and the development of the diagnostic tools that have taken place in Europe and the USA are considered as universal concepts and are encouraged to be used across the world.

Berry *et al.* (1999) explain relativism as the other end of the continuum. Relativists emphasise the need to understand people on their own terms without imposing any value judgements or prior knowledge of any kind. They avoid describing, categorising and understanding others from an external cultural point of view. They view all the psychological variations across the world as purely the result of cultural differences. Relativists are not interested in the existence of similarities across different cultural groups. The only assumption of similarity that they take is that all human beings are equal and hence should be treated so. However, they do study differences and explain them to be the result of the cultural contexts in which the individual is located. Berry *et al.* (1999) comment that relativists avoid comparative studies as they are considered problematic and ethnocentric, making it impossible to compare in a valid manner. Relativists stress the need to develop psychological instruments and procedures that have been developed within the local culture. They consider the difference in findings as a result of qualitative differences – for example, 'differently intelligent' rather than 'less intelligent'. Because of the high importance placed on culture and its role in behaviour variation, theoretically relativists take an emic position. This means that the theories are developed from the perspectives of the people involved in the process. I do not think that this is a stance that is often used in the field of autism, but other researchers have suggested this position for specific psychological concepts.

According to Berry (1999), universalism is the middle position between these two. Universalism agrees that basic human characteristics are universal, but the development and display of these characteristics is influenced by one's own culture. According to Berry, the degree to which any given behaviour or characteristic is universal will be different. Developing this idea further, Berry *et al.* (1999) comment that, according to universalists, cultural factors influence the extent, purpose and direction of the development of psychological processes and how they are used. Therefore, for universalists, the main question is to find out the extent to which cultural variables influence behaviour. For this reason, universalists understand the importance of comparison but apply it with caution. They are aware that assessment procedures may require modifications to be used in a different cultural setting. They consider that universally applicable concepts can only be developed by re-formulation of the existing concepts. This gives universalists a derived etic position.

Universalists believe that quantitative interpretations can be made in areas where the phenomenon of interest is similar. Berry *et al.* (1999) provide the example of depression to explain this point. They say that in cultures that share the same concept and expression of depression, it might be possible to interpret the differences on a test of depression in a quantitative manner. However, where this is different, it may be impossible to use comparable measurements. Such qualitative differences would have to be analysed theoretically to define a common dimension that can capture these differences that can then be used for comparative purposes. Universalists aim to develop a context-free definition of psychological concepts by modifying culture-specific concepts. At the same time there is also recognition that since expression of behaviour is culture-bound, context-free measurement of certain kinds of variables may never be achieved. Therefore, researchers such as Matsumoto (1994) feel that a major goal of cross-cultural psychology should be to find out which of the human behaviours are relative and which are universal. Berry *et al.* (1999) state that a concept or a relationship can be considered as universal only when there is a theoretical ground for this, and that the theory is supported by empirical evidence.

Even within the universalist position there are differences in how each researcher takes this stance. For example, both Bennett (1986) and Wiredu (1996) say that despite the differences between various groups, there are also similarities. Wiredu (1996) describes cultural differences or particularities as accidental. Both these authors argue that it is possible to study cultures on the basis of human universals. Research that takes this position often aims to develop cross-culturally valid theories and research methods or questions about the universality of these. Taking the latter stance, Greenfield (1994) says that patterns and norms of child development are often specific to Euro-American culture and are not universals. This same argument can also be used in relation to autism.

While defining universalism Berry (1999) also proposes three possible strategies that can be used to carry out research in the universal paradigm: to test current knowledge and definitions in other cultures, to explore new aspects of the phenomena in other cultures, and to generate theories on the basis of the knowledge collated from these two steps, which can then be tested for its applicability. The position that this book takes is a universalist view. The scope of this book does not follow Berry's suggestions completely, but the next chapter attempts to explore the universality of the concept of autism by exploring childrearing practices and social behaviours in different cultures, and how these then impact the process of the diagnosis of autism spectrum. I take a universalist position as I acknowledge the social construction of labels such as 'autism'. This means that while the differences acknowledged as autism in the West are perhaps prevalent across the world, these may not necessarily have the same significance. Unless we attempt to understand these differences, it will be hard to develop a universal definition of autism. If the variations in understanding are not considered, there is a danger that cognitive theories that are developed to understand autism or good practice guidelines for supporting individuals with autism and their families will continue taking an absolutist position, which could lead to culturally inappropriate services.

A MOMENT TO PAUSE

— Before you move on to the next chapter, take a few minutes to reflect on which of the three positions outlined above you take in your understanding of autism.

— Consider why you take this position. What is your evidence that this is an appropriate position to take?

— What are the implications of this position for your own work with individuals with autism and their families?

Chapter 2

ASSESSMENT AND
—— DIAGNOSIS ——

The diagnostic process and procedures for identifying autism are firmly based within the medical model of disability, where it is assumed that the reasons for the differences observed in an individual are inherent to the person. With research suggesting that causation of autism could be based on genetic and neurological causes, it is understandable why this view prevails in the field. Even though significant progress has been made in understanding the possible causes of autism in the last few decades, we are still nowhere near to using this information to develop biological tests to identify autism. For now, autism is diagnosed based on observed behaviours of the individual. As with any behaviourally assessed condition, it is hard to have objective thresholds for identifying when an individual's behaviour would no longer be considered as typical. As a society we decide on an arbitrary definition based on the characteristics that are considered as being 'abnormal'. As can be seen from the history of the diagnostic criteria for autism, definitions of autism and co-occurring characteristics have been redefined and adjusted on a regular basis, which shows the fluidity of the criteria.

How do we then decide which characteristics are to be part of a condition such as autism? Tomblin (2006) suggests that we tend to make such decisions based on two different philosophical positions: namely, neutralism (or descriptivism) and normativism. A neutralist view develops an idea for what is considered to be typical of a population, and would consider anyone who deviates from this in some observable way to have an identified condition or disorder. From a normative perspective, while deviation from the mean, or what is deemed typical, is still considered as a difference, it only requires the attention of a clinician or other professionals if this difference is then considered to be a disadvantage within a given society. For example, if we consider that having black hair is the norm, then from a neutralist view people who have any other hair colour will be considered to be atypical or to have a disorder. From a normative perspective it can be argued that in countries such as the UK, while having hair colour other than black is considered as a difference, if you have blond hair it may be considered as a desirable difference. However, if you have red hair it is likely to lead to discrimination and bullying. As can be seen from this example, a normative perspective does not necessarily consider being different as a disadvantage unless this is the view that is held by most people within a given society. In some ways a normative perspective is similar to the relativist position discussed in the previous chapter, as it states that differences only have meaning when understood from within the social group. The views of a given society determine whether it considers the divergent characteristic as an illness, disease, disorder or a positive attribute, or even a sign of saintliness. Therefore, from a normative perspective it can be argued that psychological conditions such as autism are socially constructed based on the values a society places on specific behaviours.

Whether we take a neutralist or normative perspective, it is important that we consider cultural contexts. From a neutralist perspective this knowledge will lead to an understanding of the norms for that cultural or ethnic group, such as developmental milestones, which help in developing standardised assessment tools to identify differences or disabilities. What is important to remember is that these developed norms and tools may not be applicable to other ethnic groups as they are not based on their norms. From a normative perspective, it is important to understand the cultural context, because this will help us to understand how the differences are viewed and valued, and if the observed difference is going to disadvantage the person. It could be argued that in order to classify a set of behaviours as a condition or disability, it is likely that both these perspectives are influential. It is the normative perspective that places a value on a set of behaviours – for example, identifying good social interaction skills as typical or the norm and therefore a requirement – and those who do not have these skills may be categorised in some way (as in the case of autism). A neutralist approach provides us with a means to measure these differences in relation to their cultural context in order to establish if someone is within the identified category or not. The next section briefly touches on some of these in relation to autism, and then the rest of the chapter explores how universal these views are across the world and the implication of this for diagnostic procedures.

Diagnostic criteria for autism

The characteristics used as the basis for autism diagnosis in DSM-5 (APA 2013), the International Classification of Diseases-10 (ICD-10, WHO 1993) and most of the screening and assessment tools focus on looking at differences in the areas of communication, social interaction and repetitive, ritualistic behaviours. For those who are unfamiliar with the DSM-5 criteria for autism, here is a quick reminder:

DIAGNOSTIC AND STATISTICAL MANUAL OF MENTAL DISORDERS, 5TH EDN CRITERIA (APA 2013)

Persistent deficits in social communication and social interaction

1. Deficits in social-emotional reciprocity, ranging, for example, from abnormal social approach and failure of normal back-and-forth conversation; to reduced sharing of interests, emotions or affect; to failure to initiate or respond to social interactions.

2. Deficits in non-verbal communicative behaviours used for social interaction, ranging, for example, from poorly integrated verbal and non-verbal communication; to abnormalities in eye contact and body language or deficits in understanding and use of gestures; to a total lack of facial expressions and non-verbal communication.

3. Deficits in developing, maintaining and understanding relationships, ranging, for example, from difficulties adjusting behaviour to suit various social contexts; to difficulties in sharing imaginative play or in making friends; to absence of interest in peers.

Restricted, repetitive patterns of behaviour, interests or activities

1. Stereotyped or repetitive motor movements, use of objects, or speech (e.g., simple motor stereotypes, lining up toys or flipping objects, echolalia, idiosyncratic phrases).

2. Insistence on sameness, inflexible adherence to routines, or ritualised patterns of verbal or non-verbal behaviour (e.g., extreme distress at small changes, difficulties with transitions, rigid thinking patterns, greeting rituals, need to take same route or eat same food every day).

3. Highly restricted, fixated interests that are abnormal in intensity or focus (e.g., strong attachment to or preoccupation with unusual objects, excessively circumscribed or perseverative interests).

4. Hyper- or hypo-reactivity to sensory input or unusual interest in sensory aspects of the environment (e.g., apparent indifference to pain/temperature, adverse response to specific sounds or textures, excessive smelling or touching of objects, visual fascination with lights or movement).

The above criteria provide some specific examples of behaviour such as difficulties with pretend play, as well as more generic statements such as excessive adherence to routines. Consequently, screening and assessment tools attempt to operationalise these broad statements with specific examples of behaviour to look for. If we look at some of the popular tools used in the field such as the Modified Checklist for Autism in Toddlers (M-CHAT)

(Robins, Fein and Barton 1999), Childhood Autism Rating Scales (CARS) (Schopler and van Bourgondien 2010), the Autism Diagnostic Interview – Revised (ADI-R) (Rutter, Le Couteur and Lord 2005), and the Autism Diagnostic Observation Schedule (ADOS) (Lord *et al.* 1999), we can start to see a pattern of specific behaviours that clinicians are looking for as signs of autism. These include:

Social communication

- Failure to point with index finger to communicate

- Giving no eye contact or unusual eye contact

- Failure or difficulty in sharing interests and objects with others

- Delay or absence of speech

- Presence of echolalia or repeating of others' words

- Difficulty in appropriate use of pronouns

- Not being able to tell a narrative

- Difficulty in using and understanding non-verbal communication such as gestures.

Social interaction

- No response or delayed response to name

- Not engaging in joint attention

- Difficulty in playing with other children (joint interactive play)

- Difficulty in understanding social rules and customs

- Difficulty in initiating, sustaining and ending a conversation

- Not seeking comfort from others in case of pain or distress

- Difficulty in understanding others' emotions

- Difficulty in expressing emotions in an appropriate manner.

Imagination and rigid, ritualistic and repetitive behaviour

- Presence of self-stimulatory behaviour (such as flapping hands, rocking and spinning)

- Resistance to changes

- Unusual responses to sounds, sights and textures

- Inability to play with toys in an appropriate way – for example, tendency to line up objects

- Not getting involved in pretend or imaginative play

- Intense interest in specific topics, subjects or objects

- Developing own routines and rituals and insisting on following them

- Difficulty in understanding that others' knowledge could be different from their own.

All the screening and diagnostic tools tend to provide algorithms to calculate the likelihood of autism based on the observed behaviours and their severity. Scores above a specific figure are usually considered as indicators of autism, thereby using a neutralist position to assessment. However, as discussed above, these norms are developed and agreed based on majority behaviours in a given society. Therefore, the cultural and social expectations of society will inevitably decide which behaviours are acceptable and which are a cause for concern, that is, indicators of autism. Since these tools have been developed and standardised in North America and Western Europe, it can be assumed that these reflect the norms of these societies and therefore are valid tools for assessment in these contexts. But how universally are these behaviours considered as differences or disabilities, and what are the implications when working with individuals from minority ethnic communities?

Cultural perceptions of features associated with autism

In this section I explore how some of the above-mentioned behaviours are viewed in different cultural contexts to see if there are any issues in applying criteria developed in one part of the world to a context elsewhere in the world. There is some emerging literature specifically in the field of autism where these behaviours have been the subject of research interest, but when it comes to cultural differences, a rich source of data is also found in anthropological studies. Therefore, the following discussion uses both these sources to develop a better understanding of this issue.

Eye contact

Differences in eye contact are considered one of the classic features of autism, both in professional circles and also in the common understanding of autism. However, the quality and quantity of eye contact is culturally determined. For example, giving direct eye contact is considered to be inappropriate in Korean, Chinese and some other Asian cultures (John Lian 1996; Park 1996; Zhang, Wheeler and Richey 2006). O'Hagan (2001) mentions that among Navajo Indians giving direct eye contact is an uncommon practice. Some Nigerian and Ghanaian families I have worked with also mention that giving direct eye contact is considered rude in their culture, especially to people who are older. Carter *et al.* (2005) state that this is also the case in Kenya where children are taught not to look at elders as a sign of respect. Blais *et al.* (2008) report that similar restrictions are imposed in South Korea where giving eye contact to an unfamiliar adult is considered to be impolite. In a cross-cultural study conducted in Japan, Trinidad and Canada, McCarthy *et al.* (2006) found that out of the three groups, Japanese participants provided less eye contact when answering questions. These differences in the level of eye contact are perhaps related to the value that eye contact is given in different societies.

There seem to be differences even among different ethnic communities living in the same country. Exploring the use of eye contact in White American students compared to Black American students, Fugita, Wexley and Hillery (1974) found that White students were more likely to maintain eye contact while answering questions in an interview situation compared to Black students. LaFrance and Mayo (1976) made similar conclusions from their research, but also suggested that this increased eye contact among White Americans was more likely when they were speaking to another White person, and there was a drop in the level of eye contact when White people were interacting with Black people. The difference in eye contact was found even when two Black people were communicating with each other. It is possible that these cultural differences in the amount of eye contact provided is nurtured from a young age in some cultures. For example, Schofield *et al.* (2008) found that White American children gave more eye contact to their parents, and that this shared eye gaze was also demonstrated by their parents. This was comparatively less in Mexican American children and their parents. As mentioned above, from an autism perspective lack of eye contact is considered a key indicator of the condition. This is partly because this is deemed to be an important social skill in the European and North American majority communities. Therefore, those who do not show this behaviour are not following the norm, and potentially showing one of the signs of autism (from a neutralist position). However, from a normative perspective it could be argued that the importance and purpose attached to eye contact varies across different ethnic and cultural groups, as is evident from the above studies. Therefore, lack of or limited eye contact may not be considered as a disorder in every community. These differences could have implications for individuals from minority ethnic communities living in the USA or Europe, as it is likely that the professionals working in these countries are using the neutralist perspective based on majority community norms.

Use of gestures

Similarly, as any well-travelled person will know, using gestures and the meaning of specific gestures is also culturally determined. Zhang *et al.* (2006) mention that using an index finger to point is considered impolite within Chinese communities. As a result, children are taught not to point at objects or people. From my own upbringing, I am aware that pointing at a person is not considered polite behaviour within Indian communities either. While conducting a piece of research within a Somali community living in the UK, I became aware that using gestures is considered socially inappropriate behaviour within the community (Perepa 2014). Lack of pointing skills is considered an early red signal for autism in a number of screening and assessment tools, once again showing a predominantly neutralist perspective and largely ignoring cultural differences.

Development of speech

There also seem to be differences in expected developmental milestones across cultures. During her research in India, Daley (2004) found that parents were not worried if their son was not speaking until the age of four, as the assumed notion in Indian culture is that boys speak late. As a result, it is not considered unusual if a boy does not start speaking until four years of age. While lack of speech could be another factor to consider for autism diagnostic purposes, for these families, their sons might well be within their expected normal developmental range. Similarly, in the Wolof tribe of Africa, knowledgeable people and those of higher social class are expected to speak less (Irvine 1978). Therefore limited speech, while still acknowledged as a difference, would be considered a sign of higher intelligence or good upbringing, and not as a sign of a communication impairment.

Language development and style

Even after speech is developed, the vocabulary development and structure of language varies among different languages. Duranti and Ochs (1996) state that Samoan children are typically exposed to language related to emotions earlier than children in the USA. However, when it comes to some syntactic structures, Samoan children are at a disadvantage as adults only use these forms in formal occasions where children are not usually allowed. As a result, on a test that has been standardised in the USA, Samoan children are likely to perform way above the norm in emotional language areas, but perhaps not so in syntactic structures. Young children coming from minority ethnic communities who are bilingual or multilingual may also get confused between the language structures in the various languages they speak in the initial stages.

Differences have also been noted in the style of communication in other cultures. For example, in the Korean language the use of indirect expressions and elaborate language is common practice (Kim, Kim and Rue 1997). In such a community, using a direct style of communication would be considered as rude or inappropriate. In some African communities it is considered rude to state a belief in the first person, hence the third person is often used for commentaries (Jamin 1994). However, in Western cultures, using indirect language or referring to oneself in the third person is also associated with communication patterns displayed by people with autism.

The structure of languages across the world is different. For example, while there are no honorifics (suffixes used with verbs to denote the social hierarchy of the communication partner) in English, this is common in most other languages. It is possible that rather than the expected idiosyncratic use of language as indicated in diagnostic criteria, it is in these subtle language-specific issues that the differences of someone with autism are visible. In fact, Grinker (2007), in his research in Korea, found that clinicians often reported deficits in this area as consistent features in children and adults with autism, highlighting the role of the normative perspective in understanding the cultural significance associated with different behaviours.

Emotional expressions

Understanding and expressing emotions is considered to be part of typical human development, and which emotions to express, where and in which manner is still influenced by an individual's cultural context (Elfenbein 2013; Elfenbein *et al.* 2007). From my own experience I am aware that in some traditional Indian families it is not considered appropriate for females in the house to laugh in front of older male members of the family. In such situations, not smiling or laughing does not mean that the person is not happy, but the expression is restricted due to its social acceptability. Similarly, in the Chinese community a smile does not always indicate happiness but could mean embarrassment or feeling shy (Liu 2005). Jack *et al.* (2012) confirm this multiple use of the same expression based on their research. They found that unlike Westerners, Asians tend not to have set facial expressions to represent basic emotions. This could mean that the same emotion may be expressed by different people through a variety of facial expressions. Matsumoto (2009) comments that in some Asian cultures open expression of emotions is often discouraged. As a result, exhibiting feelings such as unhappiness or boredom in front of others is considered socially inappropriate. On the other hand, Vrana and Rollock (2002) found that compared to their White participants, Black people tend to be more emotionally expressive in their interactions.

The difference seems not to be limited to which emotions we show, and how and when to express these, but also in how we interpret facial expressions. Chua, Boland and Nisbett (2005) and Yuki, Maddux and Masuda (2007) argue that there is cross-cultural variability in how people from various countries scan and process social information, including facial cues and how they interpret facial expressions. In their cross-cultural study, Masuda *et al.* (2008) found that unlike their participants from the USA who focused only on faces to understand someone's emotional state, their Japanese participants considered the social context along with the facial expressions to interpret the meaning of these expressions. This is understandable if the cultural norm is not to be too transparent with your facial expressions to show your emotions. This could, of course, raise problems in an assessment scenario if someone from such a cultural background is presented with a picture of a face and asked to interpret the emotion without any other clues about the social context. It is likely that the individual may not be able to perform the task, which could be considered as an inability to interpret emotions, and therefore a potential sign of autism.

Pretend play

It is strongly believed in the West that it is important for children to engage in pretend play to enhance the development of their language skills, social interaction and imaginative thinking. As a result, lack of pretend play is considered to have serious consequences on the overall development of the child. Academics and researchers working in the field of Early Years and play have devised a number of developmental scales to identify if a child is at an appropriate stage of play. However, based on their research on 20 communities, Ember and Cunnar (2015) found that there was variability in the type of play that children engaged in and the objects they used. In their exploration of differences in play behaviour in White American and Korean American children, Farver and Lee-Shin (1997) found that compared to Korean American children, White American children were engaged in a lot more pretend play activities during their free time. In a follow-up study, Farver and Lee-Shin (2000) also found that Korean American children spent a greater proportion of time engaged in parallel play (46%) and solitary play (29%). In comparison, White American children spent more time in social play that involved being actively involved with their peers. Moreover, White American children were engaged more in aggressive pretend play and competitive play compared to Korean American children. Based on this information, it appears that the normal play habits of some of the Korean children would meet the diagnostic criteria for autism, and this again indicates the problem with using Western-defined criteria and applying an absolutist position to define autism.

Similarly, it emerges from Edwards' (2000) research that less than half the children in the sample observed in India were engaged in pretend play. Based on their practice, Norbury and Sparks (2013) comment that in some cultures children may not be encouraged to play with miniature toys and that they are particularly wary of dolls with moving eyes. Although they do not explain the reason for this fear, it could be that it originates in their cultural practices and beliefs such as in voodoo. Such studies then raise the question as to whether pretend play is so crucial for a child's development, and if not, where these children from Korea or India develop the skills that children in Europe and North America tend to develop via pretend play. Play skills, like other skills, are inculcated within a society. In their comparison of play in White American and Mexican American children, Farver and Howes (1993) found that mothers of White American children tend to engage in symbolic and pretend play with their children. On the other hand, Mexican American mothers tend to have a more structured style of play with their children. Lancy (2007) argues that there are also differences as to who children play with, as it is not considered to be the norm in some cultures to play with parents or other adults. This latter point has an effect on the diagnostic process, and is revisited later in this chapter.

Social interaction

Social interactions come with many subtle rules such as when to take turns and which topics to discuss. These are often culturally influenced. For example, a British sense of humour is different from an American sense of humour, although both countries speak the same language. In India friends and family members do not see anything wrong in asking questions about someone's income, which is considered to be a taboo subject in the UK. In an early comparative study, Collett (1971) states that there are differences in non-verbal interaction aspects such as body contact, body orientation, physical proximity and the volume of the voice between European and Middle Eastern people.

Knapp, Hall and Horgan (2013) state that our interaction styles are based on whether the cultural group we belong to is a high-context one or a low-context one. If a cultural group is more context-dependent (such as the Asian communities mentioned above), there is more emphasis on indirect and implicit communication, whereas in low-context cultures the emphasis is on verbal communication. For example, in her research on parental perceptions of autism in India, Daley (2004) found that initial concerns for Indian parents were usually the social difficulties that their child has, rather than speech delays, whereas parents in the USA tend to be alerted about their child's difference based on lack of language skills or general developmental delay. It is possible that these differences in parental reports are based on whether they are high-/low-context cultures.

The difference is not just in how to interact but also with whom to interact. Based on their research, Carter *et al.* (2005) say that in Kenya it is considered unusual for a child to sit and talk to an adult. Expanding on the idea of a cultural basis for observed behaviour, Wilder *et al.* (2004) add that behaviours such as lack of normal attachment to family members, poor social interaction and communication skills, and lack of emotional expression, all have their roots in cultural differences and expectations.

Stereotypical behaviours

There seems to be variance even in the characteristics of individuals who have been identified with autism in different parts of the world. For example, reviewing the limited amount of research about autism in Africa, Ametepee and Chitiyo (2009) state that few of the studies have reported that stereotypical behaviours associated with autism, such as rocking or hand flapping, were not as common in children diagnosed with autism in Africa. They do not provide any further information as to whether other sorts of repetitive behaviours are prevalent in these children, but this does raise the question as to which behaviours are associated with autism by clinicians in Africa, because, as per DSM-5 (APA 2013), stereotypical behaviour is part of the diagnostic criteria.

One of the first comparative studies between individuals with autism in Africa (Ghana, Nigeria, Kenya, Zimbabwe, Zambia and South Africa) and the UK conducted by Lotter (1978) provides some answers to this. He found that there was a difference in behaviour patterns exhibited by individuals with autism in the UK compared to those from African countries. Lotter found that children living in African countries were more likely to engage in specific movements such as twisting objects, carrying them and banging them, while children from the UK engaged in more 'classic' autism behaviours such as flapping, self-aggression and being engaged in ritualistic play. This does raise the question as to whether behaviour patterns associated with autism are culture-specific.

Cognitive styles

Studies in the last decade or so have moved away from just looking at specific characteristics or behaviours for autism to understanding if there are any differences in cognitive styles of individuals across the world. Masuda and Nisbett (2006) and McKone et al. (2010) argue that there is a difference in the way we attend to visual stimuli based on our ethnicity. They suggest that while people from Western cultures have a narrow-focused attention style, where they pick up the important elements in a situation with a view to analyse these, individuals from Asian cultures are more likely to look at information in a holistic way with a view to making sense of the relations among the different objects.

Kitayama *et al.*'s (2003) research provides some evidence for this. They found that American adults performed much better on the Rod and Frame task[1] (Ji, Peng and Nisbett 2000) and its modified versions, which assess perception, compared to East Asian adults. This leads them to suggest that Americans are more field-independent than Asians, meaning that Americans pay less attention to contextual information while analysing a situation.

Based on the performance of individuals with autism in embedded figure tests, research (Jarrold, Gilchrist and Bender 2005; Pellicano *et al.* 2005; Shah and Frith 1983) suggests that those with autism are more likely to have a field-independent style of visual attention. This helps in having a more analytical approach, which seems to be the case with most individuals in the Western world compared to people from Eastern Asia. However, field-independence in autism is considered to have a physiological origin related to abnormalities in brain development (Pellicano *et al.* 2005) or influenced by gender. On the other hand, research from an anthropological basis suggests that a visual processing style, whether it is field-independent or field-dependent, is based on the social structure and social practice of a given society. Nisbett (2003) suggests that people living in an interdependent culture, such as families in Asia or Africa, will need to pay more attention to relationships and contexts, thereby encouraging them to develop a field-dependent processing style. By contrast, people living in a less interdependent community, such as in Europe or in North America, do not need to pay the same

---

1   Rod and Frame is a psychological test that evaluates how much an individual is dependent on external cues when faced with a visual perception activity.

attention to the context and relationships, which perhaps leads to a more field-independent processing style.

Does this mean that individuals with autism from Asian cultures are less likely to have a field-independent style of processing? Koh and Milne (2012) explored exactly this in their study where they compared cognitive styles in people with and without autism in the UK and Singapore. According to their research, while there was a marked difference between the visual processing style of people with and without autism in the UK, this was not apparent among participants in Singapore. This is one of the first studies to explore some of the cognitive theories associated with autism and question their universality. If further studies confirm these results, this suggests that current diagnostic tools that are based on these assumptions may not be appropriate to be used with people from some cultures.

The above discussion highlights that a number of key behaviours associated with autism are culturally determined, and are mainly based on the Western norms (using both neutralistic and normative perspectives). Depending on the background of the family, it is possible that some families would consider that the behaviour of their child or family member is part of the normative curve and may not necessarily consider these as indicators of a disability. For example, Mandell *et al.* (2002) state that in some cultures when a child does not respond to their parent's requests it is considered that the child is strong-willed rather than considering this as an early indicator of a disability, such as autism. Information from these limited number of studies is challenging the idea that the behaviours associated with autism are universally agreed as differences or deficits. Therefore, it is important to consider the neutralistic and normative values associated with these behaviours in different ethnic groups to develop a universal understanding of autism. The following sections of this chapter will explore the implications of taking an absolutism stance on the assessment and diagnostic process.

Impact on diagnostic procedure

If the assessment and diagnostic tools for autism are based on Western norms and have been standardised on individuals from the majority communities in their countries, then using such standardised tools with individuals from minority ethnic communities is fraught with problems. Perhaps this is the reason that research suggests that children from minority ethnic communities are likely to receive their diagnosis significantly later than children from a Caucasian background (Liptak *et al.* 2008; Mandell *et al.* 2002). In addition to the content of such tools, familiarity with the test material and the procedure of tests can all impact on the reliability of the diagnosis (Carter *et al.* 2005). There might also be differences in how the family perceives the associated behaviours. This will have implications as to the reliability of the autism diagnosis, as interviews with family members are often part of the diagnostic procedure. As discussed above, from a normative perspective, identifying a difference does not necessarily mean that communities across the world will associate the same meaning or value with the observed behaviour. Along with ethnicity, other factors such as education of family members, their financial status and their attitudes towards disability and its causation can all impact on how the family perceives the differences and how much importance they place on these differences.

In countries such as the USA where access to health services are not free, the family's economic status could have an impact on whether they receive a diagnosis for their child or not (Mandell *et al.* 2002). As the percentage of families from some minority ethnic communities belonging to poorer economic backgrounds is higher, this can then impact on their access to diagnosis. Even when finances are not an issue, families' views about which behaviours are considered as typical and age-appropriate can impact when the child is referred for an assessment. For example, Mandell *et al.* (2002) suggest that African American parents are more likely to describe behaviours associated with autism as disruptive behaviours, whereas Caucasian parents tend to describe these as idiosyncratic or socially odd behaviours. Similarly, Ratto, Reznick and Turner-Brown (2016) found that, depending on the ethnic background of the parents, the behaviours that they are likely to report might vary. The Latino American mothers in their research were nine times more likely than White American mothers to report their child's temperament as the cause of concern, although both sets of parents are also likely to report speech and language difficulties as part of their concerns. Based on this, it can be hypothesised that children from some minority ethnic communities are likely to receive other diagnostic labels such as social, emotional and mental health difficulties rather than autism based on parental reports.

Parents may also prefer one label to another based on their own perceptions about different labels. For example, in Korea, where they diagnose reactive attachment disorder (RAD), which is based on similar behaviour patterns to autism, parents prefer the label of RAD because it is believed that there is a treatment for RAD, which is not the case with autism (Grinker 2007). It is considered that children develop RAD because of poor attachment with parents and therefore questions the parent's parenting skills (especially the mother's). Nevertheless, it does not have a similar impact on the whole family to autism that is considered to have a genetic basis and could stigmatise the whole family and potentially influence the marriage prospects of relatives. Cultural attitudes towards disability can also impact on whether the family would like to seek help or not. For example, in some communities having a child with a disability could be seen as a result of a family's misdeeds (Dyches *et al.* 2004). The impact of family attitudes towards disability in accessing services is discussed in more detail in the next chapter.

There is a range of possible reasons that influence how quickly a child will receive a diagnosis of autism. Liptak *et al.* (2008) report that children from minority ethnic communities in the USA receive their diagnosis for autism significantly later than White American children. They argue that this seems to be the case irrespective of the SES of the family. Since the diagnostic label is often related to access to services in the UK and USA, this would also have implications for accessing services for support for the individual and their family members. However, not all the differences are necessarily the result of family views and attitudes alone; the diagnostic criteria and process will also need to be considered as part of the holistic picture.

Implications for assessment/ diagnostic items

Great emphasis in most of the standardised screening and assessment tools for autism is on social communication skills such as eye contact, use of gestures and other non-verbal communication means, and providing narratives. As the above discussion highlights, all of these aspects are influenced by the cultural norms of the individual, which can impact the assessment of autism in individuals coming from a minority ethnic community. There is increasing research which suggests that there is potential cultural bias in the assessment items in some of the standardised tools. For example, Matson *et al.* (2011) conducted a cross-cultural study of autism symptoms in children from the USA, Israel, the UK and South Korea. They found that individuals in the UK performed significantly worse in all domains (non-verbal communication, verbal communication, restricted interests and socialisation) compared to the other three countries. Children from Israel, on the other hand, showed fewer signs of impairments in these areas. Freeth *et al.* (2013) conducted another comparative study between typical students in higher education in the UK, India and Malaysia who were asked to complete the Autism Spectrum Quotient (AQ) questionnaire (Baron-Cohen *et al.* 2001). They found that students in India and Malaysia scored higher on the AQ compared to British students. They suggest that while the AQ might be culturally sensitive to some extent, for example in relation to gender differences, it is not sufficiently accurate in identifying autism in non-European ethnicities. In fact, there is a strong likelihood that there will be an artificial increase and/or decrease in the prevalence of autism because of inappropriate assessment tools.

Looking at different communities from various ethnic backgrounds living in the same country, Chaidez, Hansen and Hertz-Picciotto (2012) found that compared to White American children with autism, those from minority ethnic communities are likely to have a different symptom profile. These children are more prone to receiving lower scores in language and communication abilities as well as lower cognitive scores. Reporting similar differences in the symptomology of White children compared to Black children, Sell *et al.* (2012) comment that children from White ethnic backgrounds are more likely to follow non-functional routines and tend to focus on parts of objects, whereas Black children with autism are less likely to show such attention to detail or display similar routines. This further raises the issue of potential cultural bias in the characteristics that are being considered as part of autism. In fact, Harrison *et al.* (2017) found that there is cultural bias for three out of the ten items included in the ADOS (Autism Diagnostic Observation Schedule). This included unusual eye contact, stereotyped use of words or phrases and immediate echolalia. They argue that Black American children are more likely to have higher scores in all these three areas. Children from Hispanic backgrounds, on the other hand, are likely to receive a higher rating only for the unusual eye contact item. This reminds us that ethnic minorities should not be considered as one group, but it is important to consider how individuals from different communities perform against the current autism criteria. It is important that as a field we need to move away from the absolutist position that we take with regards to autism diagnostic criteria and explore the universality of these characteristics. There is an urgent need to develop culturally sensitive assessment tools and not just translate tools that are standardised in the USA or Europe into a variety of languages. To develop these it is important to understand the neutralist (what is considered a norm) and the normative (if the difference is a disorder) perspectives from the respective communities.

Structure of the assessment

A clinical diagnostic situation is unusual for most children as they are in an unfamiliar situation, with an unknown adult, and perhaps completing unfamiliar tasks. However, children in the developed world and from higher socio-economic backgrounds are used to this, to a certain extent, based on experiences such as medical appointments and being part of an education system. Carter *et al.* (2005) argue that the structure of formal assessment can be particularly difficult for children from minority ethnic communities. They found that children in rural Kenya were not used to talking to an unfamiliar adult for extended periods. The cultural norms were that children did not spend too much time chatting with adults, and therefore the unusual experience of having to interact with an adult for an extended period of time could impact on the performance of the children within a test situation. Carter *et al.* (2005) suggest that children who are not exposed to a formal education system may not be used to the idea of assessment and therefore lack the motivation to engage in such activities. If this is the case, it is important that rather than asking the child to engage in activities with the adult, other children, such as their siblings, may need to be included in the activities. It may also need to be considered whether assessment should be broken into smaller activities so that the child is able to attend to the best of their abilities based on their normal social interaction patterns.

Adams (2002) argues that pragmatic skills are highly dynamic, which makes it difficult to evaluate their reliability. As mentioned above, this might be particularly the case for individuals from minority ethnic communities. The context of the assessment and age of the individual being assessed could also impact on the behaviour of the individual. For example, Norbury *et al.* (2009) conducted a study where they recorded the eye movements of adolescents with and without autism while they were watching scenes of social interaction. They found that it was not only the young people with autism who paid less attention to the eye region, but that there is a huge variance in young people who were not on the autism spectrum. This could mean that the amount of eye contact we provide is perhaps defined also by the age of the individual and the activity they are engaged with. Nadig *et al.* (2010) conducted a similar comparative study between those with and without autism. They found that the amount of eye contact increased in both groups when the topic of conversation was of interest to the person. This could have implications to a test scenario where perhaps the topic of conversation is not of particular interest to the individual, which can then impact on their eye contact.

As discussed above, the nature of play seems to be culture-specific. There are differences in how engaged parents are in their child's play (Haight *et al.* 1999) and which type of play is encouraged within any cultural context (Cote and Bornstein 2000). This means that assessment of children using play-based approaches may be challenging for the child to engage with, due to the unfamiliarity with the process, and therefore produce unreliable results. Finding alternatives to this type of assessment might be necessary for getting reliable data from some children.

Materials used for the assessment

Anyone using an assessment tool that is developed in a country other than where it is being used very quickly becomes aware that the contextual nature of vocabulary creates specific challenges while using such tools and can seriously compromise test results. This is the case even when the test has been developed in a country that shares the same language, since there are bound to be issues of vocabulary and idiom. I am aware that some of my colleagues will not use a specific test because of this; for example, words like 'vacation' or 'soccer' are not common in the UK. Some of the standardised tests have been localised to address this issue, although these may not necessarily take into consideration the needs of immigrant children who perhaps have been exposed to a different version of English to their current country of residence. For example, a child from India might be more familiar with the word 'vacation' rather than 'holiday', even though they have moved to the UK. It is also worth noting that bilingual children may perform differently depending on the language used in the assessment. Autism diagnostic tools do not always consider this.

Assessment with children often involves using toys and dolls, and there is an assumption that all children are familiar with these. Norbury and Sparks (2013) state that in their work with families from minority ethnic communities, some families reported that playing with dolls or toys was unusual for their children as they were not familiar with these in their home situation. Similarly, picture cards are very common in assessment tools to elicit vocabulary or narratives. Carter *et al.* (2005) report that children in rural areas who may not have had access to formal education may be unfamiliar with pictorial representation and this can impact on their performance. Norbury and Sparks (2013) further argue that even when children are familiar with pictorial representations, the verbal responses provided could be dependent on the language norms of the individual. They provide the example of Puerto Rican children in the USA who responded with descriptive terms rather than nouns in a vocabulary test. Children from this community are used to defining objects by their purpose, such as an object that cuts, rather than name the object, that is, scissors. It is important for the clinicians to find out from the family what their family norms are and to select an appropriate assessment tool accordingly, to make a reliable judgement of the child's abilities.

The need for ensuring that the concepts are understood is not only relevant for the child, but also for their family members. When assessments include gathering information from family members it is important to check that the family has sufficient understanding of the language in which the interview will be conducted. Although some families may have functional language skills, this does not mean that they will have sufficient knowledge to engage in discussions involving complex concepts such as pretend play or non-verbal communication.

Relevance of the diagnosis

From a normative perspective it is important to consider whether the identified difference is causing sufficient disadvantage to the individual for it to be considered as a disability. It is likely that, while features of autism might be present in an individual, these do not have any negative impact on the individual because of their social context. Professor Rita Jordan often asks the audience in her talks, 'Would a person with autism still be considered to have autism if they are on their own on a desert island?' She raises this question to highlight the social nature of the condition. Examples of these social and cultural factors can be seen in the emerging literature. For example, Kim *et al.* (2011) conducted an epidemiological study of school-age children in South Korea and identified the high levels of autism in the country using ADOS and ADI-R. Interestingly, around 60 per cent of these children were attending mainstream school settings. As far as it can be inferred, there has been no concern about these children, nor were they referred for a psychological assessment. However, these children met the assessment criteria for autism, and Kim *et al.* (2011) use this to suggest there may be a great number of undiagnosed individuals with autism among the general population of South Korea. While it might be the case that there are individuals who would meet the assessment criteria for autism, is it important to identify them as such if this does not impact their day-to-day living? From a normative perspective clinicians should look at the contextual factors of the individual and their family and consider the need for a diagnosis accordingly rather than impose their own views. There is a danger in introducing a disability where it is not considered as such within the society.

Assessors' cultural background

While it is perhaps recognised that the individual might show different behaviour because of their ethnic background, it should not be forgotten that the assessor's own cultural norms also impact the process. For example, while ADOS suggests recording unusual eye contact (Lord *et al.* 1999) as one of the aspects to consider for a diagnosis of autism, there are no agreed standards about how much eye contact is considered as 'normal' in any given situation. Therefore, the assessor is drawing conclusions on the unusual nature of eye contact based on their own personal norms, which could be very different from the person being assessed, especially if there are also differences in their ethnic background, age and gender.

There is increasing evidence to suggest that any assessor involved in psychological and language assessments is not completely objective, but brings their own cultural values, norms and attitudes. This could also include perceived views about autism, behaviours associated with the condition and the likelihood of its prevalence in different ethnic communities. For example, Begeer *et al.* (2009) found that paediatricians in the Netherlands were less likely to identify autism if the child referred to them belonged to a minority ethnic community. They suggest that perhaps this explains the under-representation of non-European children with autism in the country. Similarly, Mandell *et al.* (2002) found that children from African American backgrounds tend to receive their diagnosis for autism on average a year-and-a-half later than White American children. Children from an African American background also need three times more visits to clinicians before they receive the diagnosis. Analysing the autism records held at the CDC in the USA, Mandell *et al.* (2009) found that children from minority ethnic communities are less likely to be identified with autism compared to White American children. Is this due to the result of professional inability to recognise autism in individuals from minority ethnic communities?

There could be a variety of reasons for this failure to identify autism. It is possible that professionals are unable to differentiate between features of autism and issues arising from learning the dominant language as a second language (Lindsay *et al.* 2006). Similarly, professionals working with new immigrant families may consider the difficulties being experienced by the child in communication and social interaction to be the result of problems with adapting to the new country rather than autism (Reijneveld *et al.* 2005). It is not only the ethnicity of the family but also their SES that seems to impact professional perceptions. In their study, Cuccaro *et al.* (1996) found that professional interpretations of the presented behaviour patterns seem to be influenced by the professional training received by the individual as well as the SES of the family, with children from a poorer SES being under-identified as being on the autism spectrum.

In addition to these aspects, the ethnic background of the clinician and the familiarity of different diagnostic labels will also have an impact on which one is provided. For example, in South Korea there is a unique condition known as reactive attachment disorder (RAD). This is attributed to lack of love from the parents and poorly developed attachment with them. The behaviour patterns identified as RAD are very similar to those considered as autism in the West (Grinker 2007; Shin *et al.* 1999). Therefore it is likely that a professional from South Korea is more inclined to give the label of RAD than autism.

Final suggestions

If culture and ethnicity are so ingrained, it is hard to ignore the impact of these on our practice. However, it is important to be conscious of our own bias and beliefs, and endeavour to set these aside when working with a family. The starting point for any discussion will have to be to understand the perspectives of the individual and/or their family members. Answers to some simple questions will help you to understand this. For example, what behaviours are they worried about? Why do these behaviours cause an issue? How does this impact the individual or their family member's life? This information can then inform clinical judgements with regards to how the identified difference has a negative effect on the individual and their family. This will then help in making appropriate diagnostic decisions. Although the current diagnostic criteria cannot be changed by individual practitioners, gathering the above-mentioned information will help in reducing the cultural bias within diagnostic and assessment procedures. Engaging in such conversation will also help to explain the diagnosis to the individual and the family – for example, the behaviours and issues described by the family can be used to explain how this fits the diagnostic criteria of autism.

A MOMENT TO PAUSE

— Depending on your role, consider what steps you could take to reduce the cultural bias in the assessment and diagnostic procedures used in your setting.

— If you are not directly involved in the diagnostic procedure, how will you encourage the family or the individual to express their cultural norms to the professionals involved in the diagnostic procedure?

Chapter 3

ACCESSING
——— SERVICES ———

Public services tend to be developed in response to the needs of individuals within a particular society. Therefore, they are based on the beliefs and values of that community. Where there is diversity within a society, for example where multiple cultures and ethnicities live together, the developed services may not automatically meet the requirements of everyone. Webb (2000) argues that providing the same service to everyone is appropriate only when the needs of every person are the same. As this is not the case in most parts of the world, it is important to understand the beliefs, values and attitudes of different ethnic groups towards autism and what they consider as appropriate services and interventions. Our attitudes towards disability are often based on our views regarding the cause of the disability. Without this knowledge it is possible that the services that are developed are not culturally sensitive to the needs of all the ethnic groups living within the society. For example, whether we consider that the individual is responsible for their condition or not will have an impact on how we feel about the condition.

Views about causation

Understanding a family's views about causes of autism is important as this will usually inform their decisions regarding the interventions for the individual with autism, but can also have an impact on the overall wellbeing of the members of the family. A starting point is to find out if there is a word for 'autism' in their language. Based on my work with minority ethnic communities living in the UK, I am aware that many languages do not have a word for autism. Connors and Donnellan (1993) had this experience in their research with the Navajo Indian community, who did not even have a word for disability until acculturation into the White American society took place. Of course, it is likely that people within the Navajo community recognised differences, especially with physical disabilities, but perhaps the value placed on these differences was not equivalent to the concept of disability. Not having a term to describe the condition of autism can make it harder to understand what it is, as there is no history of the condition within that culture. This means that the individual and their family have to make sense of a whole new concept. Some languages have started using the English word 'autism' in their own language. While this is a practical solution as it provides the community with comparable information from other parts of the world, this would still involve a steep learning curve as there is no history of the concept in their own language. As a result, some of these cultures compare autism with intellectual disabilities or mental health issues based on their own interpretation of the observed behaviours. These perceptions will have implications in terms of the services the individual and their family members consider as appropriate for themselves and therefore which of these they access.

Different perceptions regarding milestones

We often assume that all children achieve developmental milestones at the same period and that this view is shared across the world. As has been seen in the previous chapter, this information is also used to diagnose autism. As I have already stated in that chapter, this does not seem to be the case, and some communities may have different understandings of when specific developmental milestones should be reached. Ratto *et al.* (2016) conducted a comparative study where they asked mothers of children with autism from White American and Latino backgrounds to estimate when children achieve different milestones. They report that the estimates provided by both sets of parents were significantly different from the expected norms. While the White mothers were behind in their estimates by around three months, Latino mothers were even more behind, by four months. This was especially the case in the area of adaptive skills such as toilet training and getting dressed. This means that some families from minority ethnic groups may raise concerns about their child's atypical development at a much later age than what would be considered as the norm. This would have implications in terms of getting a diagnosis and accessing services, as both of these might be delayed. In fact, it is possible that by the time the family raises concerns and receives a diagnosis, they are no longer eligible for some of the early intervention programmes. We will explore the implications of this in the next chapter.

Differences in expectations regarding developmental milestones along with lack of diagnostic labels could be a reflection of the flexibility of a given society, one that perhaps is more accepting of human diversity. Cappiello and Gahagan (2009) comment that when a community looks at human worth in a more holistic way or attaches value to spiritual wellbeing rather than physical or intellectual abilities, it is likely that developmental differences do not carry similar significance. If the focus of a society is on individual achievement and productivity (as in most Western societies), then achieving developmental milestones is more important. If the cultural norm is to look at the whole family productivity as a measure for economic and social success, then there may be more flexibility on what is expected from an individual. Dyches *et al.* (2004) state that this emphasis on family cooperation is more prevalent in minority ethnic communities such as African American, Latino and Native American people living in the USA, which could result in more positive attitudes towards disabilities.

Role of religion

When the differences are considered as a disability, most traditional communities tend to understand the cause of autism or any other disability based on religious interpretations. In an ethnographic study in the USA of 20 Indian families who have a child with intellectual disabilities, Gabel (2004) found that most parents felt that disability was a result of sins committed by them or their child in their previous life. They considered that God had given them a child with a disability because their child and/or they had lessons to learn. Being successful in learning lessons in this life was seen as an opportunity to be released from the cycle of death and rebirth. In a previous study, Groce and Zola (1993) also found similar views among the Indian families they involved in their research. Evidence suggests that this view of autism as a consequence of sins or as a punishment from God for sins committed in a previous life is also prevalent in Puerto Rican parents (Rogers-Adkinson, Ochoa and Delgado 2003). It seems that these views of disability are based on a combination of religious and cultural beliefs that are sometimes shared by a whole community. Dobson and Upadhyaya (2002) echoed these views in the UK, where lay people from the South Asian community they interviewed felt that autism was the result of sin or a punishment from God that needed to be borne. This shows that the view held by the parents is also shared by the wider community. Therefore, how a family understands and interprets autism is not in isolation but is based on a shared community perception of the condition. If the whole community considers that autism is a result of sins committed in a previous life, then their attitude towards the individual with autism and their family will be based on this view, which could also have implications for the family in accessing services provided outside their community. It is likely that such a family may decide to hide their family member with autism rather than seek support.

Cimpric (2010) reports that, in Sub-Saharan Africa, children with autism are generally considered to be possessed by spirits or are seen as witches. This view leads to a negative perception of these children within the community. Gona *et al.* (2015) also reported similar views held by a range of people in Kenya. They thought that autism was a result of evil spirits, witchcraft or a curse put on them by someone else. Groce and Zola (1993) and Rogers-Adkinson *et al.* (2003) found that these views of disabilities being caused by the evil eye or the result of someone else's curse is also shared in Latin American, Mexican and Haitian families living in the USA. Some of these views about being a witch or possessed by an evil spirit put the blame for the condition on the individual and the family, and their community may pursue interventions based on these perceptions of the condition.

Jegatheesan *et al.* (2010b) conducted another ethnographic study with Muslim families who have a child with autism and are living in the USA. Some of the families in their study thought that their children were a gift from Allah and that God had chosen them to give them this child. Some fathers thought that their child had been given to them as a test of their spiritual and moral strength, and that God would judge them based on their performance. There was a slight difference between the different sects of the Muslim community, with the Shia Muslim parents feeling that they had a child with autism because they may have owed each other a favour or some kind of unfinished business that needed to be completed in this life. Mothers from this sect felt that their job was to help them reach salvation. It seems that religion provides these families with a sense of strength and comfort, and as such plays an important role in accepting the diagnosis of autism. Tait and Mundia (2012), in their research with parents in Brunei, found that, based on their Islamic faith, some parents considered that Allah had given them a purpose by bestowing on them a child with disabilities. Similar to parents in Jegatheesan *et al.*'s (2010b) study, these parents also considered that having a child with autism was an opportunity to reaffirm their Islamic faith. A study exploring the views of un-Orthodox Jewish Israeli families who have a child with autism found similar views (Shaked 2005). The 20 families who took part in the research felt that their child had been selected to complete an important religious mission. They also considered that their children had a higher spiritual status because of their pureness. The Navajo tribe shared this view and considered an individual with a disability to be a preacher of the tribe who has been sent to provide the clan with special lessons (Connors and Donnellan 1993). Bevan-Brown (2004) found that, in the Māori community as well, parents considered their child with autism to be a special gift to them.

Although the above studies seem to suggest that similar views are held by a whole community, this may not always be the case. In fact, the results from two studies that Skinner *et al.* (1999, 2001) conducted to understand the views of Latino mothers who have a child with developmental disabilities prove just this point. Out of the 250 mothers who took part in this study, 55 per cent stated that they believed that their child was a sign from God. While the majority of these parents saw this as a positive sign from God, such as considering it as a blessing or an opportunity to be better human beings, 3 per cent felt that they had a child with disabilities because God wanted to punish them for their sins. This research provides an example to highlight that while parents from a community could all be religious, how they interpret having a child with autism will be based on their own understanding of their religious principles. It is important, therefore, to understand the way each family interprets autism based on their religious beliefs, and not to assume that a whole community holds a similar view based on work with a few members from that cultural or religious group.

Other causational factors

Beliefs about causation of autism or any other disability are not only based on religious faith, but other cultural views influence these causational theories too. For example, in their research into the views of lay South Asian people living in the UK regarding autism, Dobson and Upadhyaya (2002) found that some people believed that autism could be passed by touch, or that this was the result of neglectful parenting or single parents. These views are perhaps held because of the limited understanding of autism within these communities, but such perceptions still influence how individuals with autism and their families will be treated within the community.

It would be incorrect to assume that families from minority ethnic communities only hold non-scientific views for the causation of autism. Gona *et al.* (2015) found in their research that while some Kenyan families believed in religious causes, other families associated biomedical reasons for the causation of autism. These included genetics and exposure to harmful materials. Gona *et al.* argue that it is simplistic to assume that these families had one way of thinking about the causes of autism, as some families held different sets of beliefs and sought interventions accordingly. In an older study conducted with Mexican American parents by Trotter and Chavira (1997), they report that these parents felt that while doctors could address the biological difficulties that an individual had, it was only the spiritual healers who could address the spiritual aspects of an illness. In their study with Indian families, Ravindran and Myers (2012) also found some families holding views that could be considered based on their Indian cultural norms, while others had a more 'Western approach' regarding causational theories. These different levels of conformity with Western views and attitudes could be a reflection of the families' acculturation process, with families who are more assimilated into the wider Western community holding views that reflect this. In my own work with families from minority ethnic communities I have often found that families hold more than one theory of causation. For example, parents may believe that it is caused because of their sins as well as considering that diet has an impact on their child's behaviour. These families did not see any conflict in holding these different views, and pursued services based on these different worldviews of autism.

Implications for the families

Families who think having a child with autism is due to God's intervention, whether as a punishment or a reward, tend to make decisions with regards to autism and how to deal with it accordingly. In their study of South Asian Muslim parents, Jegatheesan et al. (2010a) found that families who thought they were chosen by God to look after a child with autism felt that they could not complain of any difficulties they had in looking after their child as doing so would be challenging God's will. This was similar to the experiences I had with some of the families I worked with, who felt that requesting support for the individual with autism in their family would be somehow contrary to God's trust in them as a family to look after the individual. This means that the family may not access any support because they feel that they should not do so. Religious beliefs may also impact on other decisions that families make. For example, several of the Muslim families I worked with would not access a source of funding in the UK that had been generated by lotteries. This reflects the Muslim belief that playing the lottery is considered as gambling, and this renders the fund *haram*, or of an impure source.

This could create difficulties if there were no alternative sources of funding to support the family. If the community considers a person with autism as a saint or as the voice of God, this could, again, impact their views on accessing services. People from such communities might feel that having any interventions for the individual would interfere with the purpose that God has set for the individual.

Those who consider having a child with autism to be a result of sins committed by either the parents or the individual with the condition may feel that there is no point in seeking help, as God's intention is to punish them. Therefore, they may have the attitude that they need to bear the difficulties as this is the only way for them and the individual with autism to make up for the sins they committed in their previous lives and to break out of the cycle of rebirth. It is also possible that the family may consider it their duty to look after the person with autism as part of their penitence. Therefore, accessing services such as respite (short break schemes) or even developing the individual's independence skills could be considered as contrary to what is expected from them by God. As I mentioned above, it is possible for a community to have both positive and negative views about disability at the same time. For example, in the Navajo community an individual with any illness or disability receives ceremonies that are aimed at curing the person. At the same time, when an individual goes through the ritual they are also accepted by the community. Connors and Donnellan (1993) state that, due to this view, within this community no value judgement is placed on behaviours such as spinning or flapping.

Some researchers suggest that parents' religious beliefs could also have an impact on how they cope with having a child with autism. For example, Rogers-Adkinson *et al.* (2003) found that parents from a Colombian, Mexican or Puerto Rican background who had strong religious beliefs were more accepting of their child's condition and the limitations that this may impose on them compared to White American parents who were less religious or who had no faith. They argue that this acceptance can be interpreted by professionals working in the field as resistance to access services or implement interventions. What is required instead is awareness that the same behaviours do not produce a similar impact on every family. It is also important that even though accepting autism as a result of God's wish (the so-called magical model of disability) may seem unusual to some people, this might be a perfectly normal world vision for others. Therefore, understanding and accepting this view is crucial to develop any kind of services for such families, and also for developing mutual trust with these families.

Attitudes towards autism

As discussed in Chapter 1, the conceptualisation of autism is based on Western norms. As a result, it is possible that within some communities these characteristics are not considered as a disorder or a disability at all. In fact, in a piece of research I completed (Perepa 2007), a number of families from African and Asian backgrounds living in the UK were suggesting that the behaviours that signify autism in the UK would not be considered a disability in their country of origin. This could be because these communities had a broader category of normal behaviour or that there was limited awareness of autism. One implication of this is that the family and the community might struggle with accepting the label of autism and may challenge it. It is likely that people within the community might advise ignoring the guidance being provided by the professionals as the issue was not serious enough or that the child would outgrow the difficulties. It is also likely that these perceptions would lead the family to experience autism in a different way. For example, in a comparative study of White American and African American mothers who have a child with autism, Bishop *et al.* (2007) found that African American mothers reported lower levels of perceived negative impact of having a child with autism compared to White American mothers. Bishop *et al.* conjecture that this difference in perception is perhaps a reflection of how impairments are viewed in a society based on their own cultural belief systems.

Awareness of autism within a community has a major impact on the attitudes towards the condition and its characteristics. Salm and Falola (2002) report from their research that in African communities, where it is expected that elders and male members of the community command respect, when a child with autism is not following instructions because of their difficulties in communication, this could be interpreted as disobedient and disrespectful behaviour. Similarly, Bevan-Brown (2004) found in her research in Māori attitudes towards autism that while some families were accepting of the difference, others were avoided by their extended families because of their child's behaviour, which was caused by the limited understanding of autism within the community. Some community members found it hard to understand a hidden disability and would often comment that there was nothing wrong with the person. These views are not specific to the Māori community, and have been well documented in the literature related to autism and family experiences in several countries. In some other communities disabilities might be seen in a more negative light. For example, Kleinman (1986) reports that the Chinese participants in their research felt that a person with chronic illness or disability did not have the same rights as someone who was healthy. If such a view is held in a community, it is possible that people within that society do not feel that the person with autism should have access to appropriate services or should strive for similar goals as a person without a disability.

Attitudes are also informed by the general values held within a society. In societies where a child's achievements and their behaviour are considered to be a reflection of the parents and may affect the wider family's standing and reputation, it is important for the family that the child excels in areas valued by the community such as education, social etiquette or extra-curricular activities. In such a society, having a child with autism could have different implications for the family, as it does not provide them with an opportunity to showcase how effective they are as parents or how good they are as a family. Hyun Uk Kim (2012) suggests that such social stratification is the norm in Korea. This means that the family not only has to support their family member with autism, but also deal with the lower social status they may have as a result of this. This can make it particularly hard for the families to cope with a diagnosis of autism or to support the individual with autism. In some communities, having a member of the family with a disability such as autism also has implications on the perceptions of other family members. For example, they may be considered to be less intelligent or may find it difficult to get married because of the fear that getting married into such a family would lead to having a child with autism in their own family. Therefore, it is not just parents but also the siblings and cousins of the person with autism who may be judged based on the incidence of autism within their family.

It appears from this discussion that having autism within some minority ethnic communities only leads to negative perceptions and experiences. The limited amount of research there is about the experiences of families from different ethnic groups with a child with autism suggests that there is no single view that can be applied to all communities. For example, in their study, Jegatheesan *et al.* (2010a) found that the South Asian Muslim families who were part of the research expected full inclusion of their child with autism into social life. They felt that it was important for their child to learn to mingle with a wide range of people including extended family and friends. As different generations are likely to speak different languages, these families also wanted to bring up their children as multilingual, as this was necessary for their social inclusion, and found it frustrating when professionals were advising them to use only English as a means of communication. They felt that by doing so they were denying their child an opportunity to be part of their own wider family and ethnic community. It could be argued that South Asian families also placed similar emphasis on social stratification, as suggested by Hyun Uk Kim above, and yet these parents seemed to have different attitudes towards their child's autism.

The knowledge and understanding of autism within the family and wider society will also have an impact on attitudes towards autism. We can see this in a study by Ratto *et al.* (2016) who found that Latino mothers had significantly less knowledge of autism compared to White American mothers. They thought that this was particularly significant considering that all the mothers in the research had a child who had been diagnosed with autism at least four years prior to this research study. While they do not provide any further details on why this difference is present, it could be hypothesised that this is perhaps a consequence of the limited amount of information about autism available in community languages for parents living in countries such as the USA, Australia or the UK. This means that families from such communities are basing their approaches to autism on their existing knowledge, which might be limited, especially if the language also does not have a word for autism, and they also form attitudes based on this knowledge.

It is important to understand that there are many factors that contribute towards the perceptions of autism within a specific family or community. These could include severity of autism, financial resources that the family has access to, where the family lives and the physical environment of the house and the neighbourhood, work commitments of the family members, and legislation in the society. All of these, along with religious and cultural factors, contribute to the experience of autism for an individual or their family. In their study of African American and White American mothers, Bishop *et al.* (2007) found that in both the groups parents were more likely to have negative perceptions of caring for a child with autism if their child had lower adaptive behaviour and had more restricted and repetitive behaviour. Along with these individual specific characteristics it also made a difference based on how many children the family had and how much support the family received from the wider community. This provides evidence for the complexity of the situation and that it should not be assumed that a family would have a specific perception based on their ethnicity or religious affiliation alone. The wider social networks and sources of support also play an important role with regard to family attitudes and aspirations.

It is important not to make assumptions based on our own pre-conceived notions. For example, it is easy to assume that parents who are well educated are likely to have a more positive attitude towards autism because of their better knowledge of the condition. However, Themba and Lord (2012) found in their study that African American mothers with lower levels of education reported lower levels of negative impact of having a child with autism compared to more educated African American or White American mothers. Trying to explain the reason for this difference, Themba and Lord suggest that mothers who had a higher education (and therefore perhaps a better SES) are likely to have higher aspirations for their child. When the child is unable to meet these expectations, this could lead to higher levels of disappointment, which then impacts on parental attitudes. Dilworth-Anderson *et al.* (2005) suggest that African American parents with lower education are more likely to follow the traditional family patterns where looking after one's own family is considered an important duty. It is possible that this belief could mean that the parents and other family members assume that looking after this child with autism is part of their duty towards their family. Yet another alternative explanation could be that mothers coming from lower socio-economic background already experience a range of other stressors, and having a child with autism may not be perceived as a greater stress compared to those that impact the survival of the family, such as lack of finances or employment opportunities.

Exploring such contradictions further, Farmer *et al.* (1997) found in their research that contrary to what we would assume, parents who have access to a wider range of services and used these regularly reported higher levels of negative perceptions about having a child with autism. They propose that it is likely that families who perceive having a child with a disability are more likely to fight for better services, which explains their negative perceptions, whereas parents who are less stressed about having a child with autism are also likely to access fewer services. If these findings can be generalised, it could be argued that families from minority ethnic communities that are not accessing services are perhaps more content with their child based on their expectations from their child and what they consider their role as parents or family members. While such generalisations are tempting, caution should be applied when interpreting the results of a research study.

Issues in accessing services

As can be seen from the discussion around causation and attitudes, there are multiple worldviews when it comes to how autism is understood and perceived in various cultures. These differences will also influence what individuals with autism and their families consider as barriers to accessing services. Cultural views held by specific communities or religious groups can cause a barrier in accessing services. As discussed, where the family or the community does not acknowledge the concept of autism, they may not necessarily seek services for it. Or if the expected ages for developmental milestones vary, they may miss out on access to some of the early intervention services. If autism is seen as a result of divine intervention (whether in a positive or a negative way), accessing generic education, health or social care is not considered to be a priority or appropriate resolution by some families.

Evidence suggests that families from minority ethnic communities who are also recent immigrants are likely to be unaware of the services available to them (Perepa 2007). This could be because the nature of support available in their country of origin might be very different to what is available in their host country. They may also misunderstand the purpose of different services. General misperceptions, such as that social workers are likely to take away their child, are also held in some minority ethnic communities. Hatton *et al.* (1998) argue that there is a link between service take-up and the family's ability to speak the majority language. They argue that families who have the appropriate language skills are able to access better services irrespective of the needs of their family member. Lack of understanding of the majority language could have all kinds of implications for the family as most of the information tends to be in that language, whether it is printed, audio visual or provided in a training session. If the family does find information within their community language, it tends to not move further than an introduction to autism. While information about autism is produced in a number of languages across the world and is now easily accessible on the internet, families are still not provided with an understanding of how autism is viewed in their host country and what services are available for them. This means that there might be a discrepancy in how the family understands the condition and how it is perceived in their country of residence.

Some services have started using interpreters for supporting families during meetings or training sessions, although the interpreters will not always have the appropriate understanding or levels of subject language to help in such complex discussions. In my own work, I have found that translated information about autism in various languages often described autism as a mental illness or intellectual disability. Such information is likely to spread even more misunderstandings rather than provide appropriate knowledge. And even if a knowledgeable interpreter is available, the family may not always be willing to share personal information with a 'non-professional'. This might cause a particular issue if the ethnic community in the locality is small and it is likely that people know each other within the community. The family might feel that disclosing their issues in front of the interpreter would lead to advertising about them in the whole of their community. Another issue I found with using interpreters in my practice was when the family came from a conflict zone. This may cause difficulties if the interpreter comes from the opposite side of the conflict in their home country to that of the family. I have had family members requesting me not to have the interpreter as they were worried about their own safely and felt very vulnerable having to depend on this person.

There is an assumption in most countries that families from minority ethnic communities tend to 'look after their own'. Some researchers (such as Thomas *et al.* 2007) have also found evidence to support this claim, and suggest that these families do not access services because they tend to depend on their extended family members and friends for support. This seems a plausible explanation, especially when we look at the idea of the collectivist nature of some communities. This might be true in the case of more established ethnic communities, where it is likely that other members of the family live in the same country, but not for all minority ethnic groups. In fact, in my work in the UK I have often come across families who had no other relatives in the country. As mentioned in Chapter 1, some families were also unaware of any other parents with a child with autism in their ethnic group. This meant that these families were often more isolated, since services perceived that they were not approaching them because their needs were being met within the community.

There has been some research that suggests that families from minority ethnic communities may not access services because, along with linguistic needs, they also do not meet their cultural or religious needs. In fact, Nadirshaw (1998) argues that some minority ethnic families choose to withdraw from services because they feel that their needs are either being ignored or made fun of. These needs could be very simple – for example, an individual with autism who does not want to be part of a mixed swimming session, or a family that does not want to use residential care for the person with autism as they prefer looking after them in their home setting. The differences in perceptions of what is considered as important between parents and professionals has been suggested by other authors. This is partly dictated by the values we associate with different skills, attitudes and knowledge. It has been suggested that families from South Asian backgrounds tend to be collectivists and pay more attention to family ties (Chan 1986). It is therefore important for such a family to look after their family members within their home or at least be involved in the care of the individual. Because of the collectivist nature of their society, they may prefer to have other members of family included in the discussions. Hatton *et al.* (2004) argue that there are differences based on culture in terms of communication style, the perceived role of parents and professionals, and what is considered adequate information from the professionals. When there is disparity between these, it is possible that families will feel that they are being ignored or ridiculed, as Nadirshaw (1998) suggests.

Exploring other reasons for the under-utilisation of services by certain ethnic groups in the USA, Thomas *et al.* (2007) argue that some ethnic groups are less likely to access professional services because they feel that the professionals lack cultural competency. They also report that there is an overall mistrust in the system with an assumption that there is institutional discrimination. This worry about professionals and services not being culturally sensitive is not entirely unfounded. Ratto *et al.* (2016) found in their research that in spite of mothers from a Latino background having concerns about their child's development around the same time as White American mothers from a lower SES, Latino mothers had more delay in receiving a diagnosis for their child. Based on the discussion around unfamiliarity with the services in the host country, it may be that this is a contributory cause of the delay. However, it is just as likely that professionals in the field are unsure about how to identify autism in these children and are therefore less responsive to the mothers' concerns. Perhaps this is partly the reason why there is under-representation of individuals with autism coming from some minority ethnic backgrounds. It has also been suggested that cultural bias could impact access to services for some families. Broder-Fingert *et al.* (2013) and Magaña *et al.* (2013) have all reported that services received by children with autism from a Latino background in the USA and their families from the state school system are inferior to those received by children and families from a White American background, even though the diagnosis might be the same in both instances. Of course, this difference may be the result of ignorance about services in families from a Latino background, but it is also likely that an unconscious bias might occur in the allocation of resources to families from minority ethnic communities. In a recent study by Angell, Frank and Solomon (2016), they reported that some of the Latino parents in their study were unable to access appropriate services even though they were well aware of the services available locally and had good knowledge of autism. They argue that the idea that a parent who wants appropriate services for their child can achieve these by fighting for them does not seem to be true when it comes to parents from minority ethnic communities living in the USA.

Angell and Solomon (2017) also found that parents in their study chose different ways of dealing with professionals based on their own individual personalities. While some of them fought for appropriate services, as suggested above, others decided to be amicable with the professionals, as they were worried that challenging the professionals might be detrimental for the good of their child. Sharing similar views, Shah (1995) suggests that some families from minority ethnic communities may not access services because they feel they are taking more than their share. This might be related to the immigration history of the ethnic group and how they think they are perceived by the majority community. It could also be related to the individual personality of the parents and how they would like to maintain relationships with the professionals and service providers. Whatever it is, the net result is that the family is unable to access the services they need.

Making services accessible

Having explored perceptions about autism and some of the potential barriers that hinder families from minority ethnic communities to access services, this final section briefly considers what measures can be taken to make all services more culturally sensitive. One of the first steps is to start with raising awareness of the condition of autism and of the support services available. If families from minority ethnic communities are not accessing mainstream services, it may be necessary to take this information about the services and autism to settings where the families are likely to be present. Depending on each community, this could range from schools, healthcare centres and places of worship to specific community-based organisations. When using community organisations it may be particularly important to raise their knowledge of autism because, as discussed above, not all communities necessarily agree on the concept of autism or its prevalence within their community. Other avenues such as using community media can also be used to raise awareness about autism and locally available services. If autism is perceived negatively within a given community, it is also important that positive messages are sent, along with using appropriate role models of what can be achieved by someone with autism.

Looking at developing accessible information about autism in the locally required languages is another step for raising the knowledge and skills of family members. Sufficient awareness about the language capabilities of ethnic communities living in the area is important so that resources are not wasted in producing material that is perhaps not accessible for those at whom it is aimed. For example, a number of families who speak Punjabi in the UK may not be able to read the language because of their immigration history. Therefore, producing only written material in the language may not reach the whole community and audio options may have to be explored. As translation is an expensive process, it is worth exploring if there is any existing material about autism that has been produced by another organisation, and perhaps signpost to these resources and invest the money in developing more advanced material. It is also important to develop material that is culturally appropriate and does not assume that issues that are relevant within the West are also issues in other communities. For example, the concept of 'refrigerated mother',[1] which is part of the Western history of autism, may not be a shared view in other cultures. Therefore, it can be confusing to be told that this theory is now not accepted within the field as a cause for autism.

When using interpreters it is important to ensure that they understand the concept of autism and whatever information is being provided. I always find it useful to spend some time with the interpreter prior to the meeting, to clarify the terminology and concepts. This provides an opportunity to deal with any misconceptions and reaffirm the importance of vocabulary being used. It may also be important to consider the gender of the professionals and family members involved, and the interpreter. For instance,

1   In the 1960s it was considered by some academics and professionals that autism was a result of poor parenting where the parent (primarily the mother) was unable to show warmth towards her child and as a result could not develop a secure bond. These mothers were called 'refrigerated mothers'.

in communities that follow traditional gender roles, it might be considered inappropriate for a female member to ask for clarification or challenge the views being expressed by a male member. If this is the case, these issues will have to be dealt with in a sensitive manner. It is impossible to know all these culturally specific requirements for every ethnic group you interact with, and it is also possible that different people from the same group will have varying needs. Therefore, what is required is being open and having a discussion with the relevant members about their needs in a non-judgemental fashion. For example, a school I was supporting that was in a very diverse community had a parents' support group that was not attended by any of the male members from the community. After having a conversation with some of the fathers, I realised that these fathers were not attending the group because it only had female members, including the facilitator, and because of the nature of the room everybody was sitting in close physical proximity. These fathers found both these aspects difficult. As an initial solution to engage these fathers, we offered a fathers' group that was also facilitated by another colleague and myself. Having this opportunity immediately changed the level of engagement from the fathers.

Paying attention to each individual in the family is also important, as it is likely that different members in the family may have different levels of acculturation into society. This also means that their needs will be different even though they may all belong to the same family, follow the same religion and share the same cultural practices. To have such an open conversation it is important to be aware of our own values and attitudes to various aspects of service provision. It is more than likely that working with families from different ethnic groups means that we, as professionals, may need to work with people who may hold a set of beliefs that we do not agree with. For example, if a family considers that autism is caused because of God's will and you yourself are an atheist, it is important that you still respect the perceptions of those you are dealing with. Similarly, gathering information about the sources of support that the family has and their concerns for their family member with autism would help in suggesting support services that are likely to meet their needs.

Evaluating the use of your service based on ethnicity and how representative this is of local demographics will also help in understanding how accessible the service is. This could then help in planning how your service can be made accessible, if this is required. This needs engagement with families, as suggested above, as well as a willingness to be flexible in service provision. For instance, if it is known that children with autism from minority ethnic communities are likely to receive a later diagnosis, it might be worth reconsidering the cut-off age for early intervention services that are provided. Following the same guidelines for all communities could be discriminatory for some ethnic groups. As the demographics of any community change on a regular basis, it is vital to remember that the needs of the different groups in the community change accordingly, and it follows that a service that was culturally appropriate at one time may no longer reflect the developing needs of the society. I would argue that developing culturally appropriate services must be an ongoing and continuous process, and being a reflective practitioner is the first step in achieving this.

A MOMENT TO PAUSE

— Reflect on your own views of a specific ethnic or religious group and how this might affect your work with the individual and their family.

— How could you engage with the individual with autism or their family members to have a better understanding of their perceptions of autism and what they consider as features of a good service?

— What steps could you take to make your own service accessible for individuals and families coming from a minority ethnic group?

Chapter 4

EDUCATION AND
— INTERVENTIONS —

Education and therapeutic interventions are considered to be the main way to support individuals on the autism spectrum, and over the past few decades a variety of approaches and strategies have been developed. There is such a wide range of interventions available for a family or a professional to choose from that there is an acknowledgement now that approaches that are based on robust evidence need to be differentiated from those that have a limited research basis. In the USA it is mandatory that only evidence-based approaches are used by professionals in their work with individuals with autism. In some other countries, such as the UK, this is not a requirement, but it is recommended in various policies that evidence-based teaching approaches be used while teaching children with special educational needs, such as autism. The evidence base of an approach is decided by evaluating the existing research-based literature for various interventions within the field of autism, and judging which approaches are considered to be effective in producing the desired outcomes. Reichow, Volkmar and Cicchetti (2008) developed specific criteria for evidence-based practice to be used in relation to autism that can be used to evaluate the efficacy of the approach based on published research. The principle of having evidence-based practice seems logical, so that precious resources are not wasted on approaches that are perhaps ineffective or harmful for the person.

While Reichow *et al.*'s criteria provide a tool for assessment, the issue with research in the field of autism is that not many studies publish ethnicity or race as part of the demographic details of the participants. Pierce *et al.* (2014) completed the first systematic analysis of some of the published autism research to examine how many of these reported the ethnicity of the participants. They examined articles published in the three main autism research journals – *Autism*, *Focus on Autism and Developmental Disabilities* and *Journal of Autism and Developmental Disabilities* – published in 2000, 2002, 2004, 2006, 2008 and 2010, to consider if details about the ethnicity of the participants was included. They found that 72 per cent of the articles did not include information regarding the race or ethnicity of the participants. When ethnicity was reported it was often not analysed in relation to research objectives and outcomes. Therefore, it is unclear what the role of ethnicity was in terms of the research focus and results. Pierce *et al.* argue that this is a limitation in existing autism literature, making it hard to generalise the findings to different ethnic groups or countries. This is especially an issue when we are talking about good practice in the field of autism or considering the efficacy of a specific strategy or intervention. This lack of attention to ethnicity is perhaps based on the absolutist position that the field of autism takes with regards to cultural or country-based differences.

However, awareness about the importance of this information is slowly growing, and West *et al.* (2016)

reviewed the report produced by Wong *et al.* (2014) that evaluated the evidence base for a variety of autism approaches. Just like Pierce *et al.* (2014) have argued, West *et al.* (2016) found that most of the studies used in this report do not provide information about the participant's race, ethnicity or nationality. In fact, only 17.9 per cent of the studies provided this information, which is lower than that reported by Pierce *et al.*'s review. The research in which ethnicity is usually mentioned focuses on group studies (28.2%) rather than single-subject studies (16.8%). West *et al.* comment that this is not surprising since the intention of most research studies conducted with a group of people is to establish whether their findings can be generalised.

Across the 408 studies that West *et al.* looked at, the percentage of people from White ethnic groups was 19.6 (which included White, European American, Caucasian, White British, Polish, Dutch, Tasmanian and New Zealander) among the 2489 participants. However, as only 73 studies provided sufficient information about the ethnicity of their participants, when the percentage of White participants in these is explored, it rises to 63.5 per cent. Participants from other ethnicities were 20.6 per cent in these 73 studies. This shows that as Pierce *et al.* (2014) have argued, research studies in the field of autism do not pay sufficient attention to the ethnicity or nationality of the participants.

The studies that reported on these data were those that mainly focused on social skills training or parent-implemented interventions, where the largest ethnic group was White. Six approaches that are considered to be evidence-based practices for intervention do not have any studies that provide sufficient information about the ethnicity or nationality of their participants. These included:

social scripts, a structured playgroup, discrete trial teaching, extinction,[1] functional communication training and the Picture Exchange Communication System (PECS). All these approaches are very popular, and four of them are based on the principles of the Applied Behaviour Analysis (ABA) approach, which is considered one of the most evidence-based approaches.

Research conducted by West *et al.* (2016) raises concerns about the claims of evidence-based practice of some of these approaches when it comes to children or young people with autism from a non-White background. If most of the studies are not reporting this information, how do we know that the strategies and interventions that are developed in North America and Western Europe are applicable or appropriate for children with autism from different cultural backgrounds and across the world? There is an assumption that what is considered as good practice for White children living in the USA and Europe is the same for all children living in different countries and coming from various ethnic backgrounds. As Owusu-Bempah and Howitt (2000) have argued in relation to psychological constructs, it would seem from looking at this Eurocentric view of autism interventions and good practice that there is also an element of cultural imperialism. It becomes hard, then, to know which approaches are appropriate or effective for using with children from minority ethnic communities. As there is very limited evidence about this in the existing literature, this chapter aims to evaluate the implications of ethnicity when supporting children with autism in some of the main areas of differences:

---

1   Extinction is a behaviour technique where the context is changed, such as removing anything that is reinforcing the behaviour, to reduce or extinguish the identified behaviour.

communication, social interaction and play skills. I draw on my own personal experiences and interpretations, as well as using research evidence, where it exists.

Communication

A number of strategies and approaches in the field of autism are based on using visual means such as written words, photographs and pictures, as it is considered that individuals with autism are visual learners. Use of symbols or pictures is also encouraged due to the assumed universal nature of these representations. In an interesting piece of research, Huer (2000) demonstrates that how we understand or perceive a symbol could be influenced by our culture. If this is the case, it is likely that when visual strategies are used with a child with autism, not all adults in that individual's life may associate the same meaning with the symbols or respond in the same way. This means that the child with autism could get confused and may not use the strategy or use it in a way that is different to what was expected by the teacher or the speech and language therapist. The first step, therefore, before using any visual strategies with an individual with autism, is to check that the meaning associated with these symbols by the professionals is also shared by the family members.

Similarly, use of alternative and augmentative means of communication (AAC), such as sign language or PECS, is common when working with children who are pre-verbal or who have limited speech. It is often assumed that all parents will be happy to use such AACs with their child with autism. In a study I completed (Perepa 2009), I found that parents from African communities were reluctant in using AACs as they felt that this would impact on the ability of their child to develop speech. In communities such as these, where the tradition has been to share information orally, development of speech may have more significance than is appreciated by professionals working in the field. Therefore, it is important to work alongside family members when developing any intervention for these to be successful.

Some of the early communication strategies also use ideas such as 'pause and burst', where familiar songs are used to engineer situations that will encourage the child to communicate by using dramatic pauses. Norbury and Sparks (2013) report that some of the families they worked with opted out of such therapy activities because these were contrary to their cultural or religious beliefs. For example, singing may not be considered appropriate in some religious and cultural groups, or it might be forbidden for men to hear women sing. Again, engaging in a dialogue with the family members to understand the appropriateness of the selected intervention within their family context could avoid such situations.

As a society becomes culturally diverse, it is likely that it is also becoming multilingual. Children with autism from minority ethnic communities are likely to be coming from families where more than one language is spoken. This bi- or multilingual nature of the home setting will have an impact on how these children are supported within an educational setting or while meeting their speech, language and communication needs. Even when the family and the child speak the majority language there might still be some differences in the way language is used – for example, the difference in Black English is well noted in the USA and the UK. It has to be understood that the occurrence of different language conventions does not necessarily mean that the child has a language difficulty. Although there is emerging research in the area of bilingualism, autism and assessment, there is very little that explores the implications of this in providing support to the child or young person.

The nature of bilingualism is complex, and experiences of children who are multilingual are affected by a variety of factors. These could include the degree of proficiency in languages, the point at which the child has started learning the languages, and the sequence of acquiring them, whether the child learned the languages in a home setting, at school or in both places, and the sociolinguistic context (Romaine 2008). Romaine (2008) and O'Toole and Hickey (2012) emphasise the role of sociolinguistic context by explaining that if one of the languages that a child is learning is a minority language that experiences a lower social status, it is likely that the child will receive limited input in that language or use it in a reduced number of environments. However, some families may still feel that it is important for the child to learn their home language or languages, as this is the only means for the child to interact with certain members in the family or to be part of their culture. In addition to this, children themselves will have varying interests in functioning in a multilingual environment. Learning new languages could also be an area of special interest for some people with autism.

Professionals often advise parents that using more than one language may be confusing for the child and will impact in developing the child's communication skills. This guidance is more likely to be provided when the child also has additional intellectual disabilities along with their autism. While some parents follow this advice, others find this very frustrating (Jegatheesan *et al.* 2010a) as it hinders their social and cultural integration within their own community. There is developing evidence that suggests that children with intellectual disabilities are nonetheless capable of learning more than one language (Roseberry-McKibbin 2007). In fact, Gutierrez-Clellen (1999) argues that children with intellectual disabilities are able to transfer their knowledge of language structure and skills from one language to another. Similarly in their research, Petersen, Marinova-Todd and Mirenda (2012) found that there was no significant difference in the vocabulary development of bilingual Chinese children in their first language and in English. What was interesting in this study was that when these children were compared with monolingual children who only spoke English, those who were bilingual had larger vocabularies than the monolingual children. Such evidence refutes the argument that learning more than one language may be harmful for children with autism.

This means that strategies need to be developed that provide children with the opportunity to maintain their home language. Some ideas are simple – for example, if visual strategies such as a visual timetable or PECS are being used with the child (once the meaning of the symbols has been agreed), it is a good idea to have the instructions or words written in the languages the child is likely to use in the school and home setting. This not only provides the child with an opportunity to generalise the learned skills in various settings, but also creates an opportunity for the child to communicate with family members who only speak the home language. However, the grammatical structure of the home language may be different from that of English, which could cause specific issues when moving on to the sentence structure stage of PECS. For example, while PECS recommends that the 'I want' card is at the beginning of the sentence, not all languages follow a similar sentence structure, which creates issues when the child reaches this stage. Similarly, languages that are not written from left to right may also create specific challenges if bilingual cards are used. As discussed above, there is not sufficient evidence on the efficacy of PECS in other cultures, as this information doesn't seem to be gathered in most research studies. In addition to this evidence, there is also a need to adapt this approach based on the structure of the various languages. Research is also required to understand the implications of these adaptations for developing communication skills in bilingual children. Similar issues appear with other AACs such as voice-generating devices. If the device that the child uses only provides output in English, it will not be as effective in a family or community setting when interacting with family members who do not speak English. This is another area that has not been researched and that needs further exploration.

It is also important to understand the communication style used within a specific culture. For example, if pointing with an index finger is considered rude in some cultures, as Zhang *et al.* (2006) suggest, it needs to be understood what other means people coming from that culture use to indicate preferences. The child with autism could then learn these skills or, in fact, if the child already uses such means, these should be acknowledged to have an equivalent communication function during the intervention phase. Similarly, understanding the norms of language and communication patterns used within the cultural context of the child will help in complementing these with communication and language patterns required in the majority language. For example, if the child is taught in their home language to describe the function of the object rather than label it, it can be explained to the child that the conventions in English are different, or if they are bilingual, teach the vocabulary in English accordingly.

The focus should not be limited to developing expressive language and communication skills; rather, equal attention should also be given to receptive language development. It is useful to have phrase books in the child's home language at the initial stages if the child is likely to respond to these better than instructions in English. These could be noted along with the student profile in the school files, and an audio recording of the pronunciation could also be kept so that different professionals who are likely to interact with the child in the educational context will be able to communicate with the child at least at a basic level. In a single case study conducted by Lang *et al.* (2011) with a four-year-old bilingual girl with autism who spoke Spanish and English, Lang *et al.* found that when the girl was provided with instructions in Spanish during the discrete trial training sessions, she showed increased correct responses, and there was a reduction in the incidence of challenging behaviour compared to when instructions were given only in English. Studies such as this provide evidence that it is important to use the home language at least in the initial stages of schooling to help the child to settle, but also to get a more realistic view of the child's abilities.

Some studies also suggest that starting a therapeutic intervention in the child's home language could also be beneficial in developing the child's ability to learn English. For example, in a longitudinal study by Seung, Siddiqi and Elder (2006), they provided an initial intervention in a child's native language of Korean for the first 12 months. Over the next 12 months, the therapy sessions slowly started including English, before finally moving to

English-only sessions. The results of the study show that the child was able to excel in both languages by using this procedure. While it is hard to expect every professional to be proficient in various languages, bilingual colleagues (where available) or the family members of the child could be included during the intervention process. The role of the speech and language therapist in such a situation is more of a mentor or guide in the initial stages of the intervention.

Working in such collaboration also helps in understanding how far the issues observed in the child are due to their autism, and which aspects are related to learning English as a second language. For example, Lee (2011) suggests that when some bilingual children with autism are struggling with specific language-based issues such as idioms or jokes, it is important to ascertain whether this is because of their autism or as a result of their limited abilities in English. This knowledge could mean that the intervention approach used with the child might have a different emphasis based on the cause of the difficulty. Not understanding these differences could mean that the child is likely to be identified with inappropriate needs. Researchers (Cummins 2000; Winter 2001) have commented that it is likely that some bilingual children are over-identified as having speech and language difficulties while others are missing appropriate support. Difficulties in assessing the needs of these children have often been quoted as the reason for this disparity. In a more recent study by Skahan, Watson and Lof (2007), they surveyed 333 speech and language therapists' opinions on their confidence levels and the nature of the assessments they use. A majority of these therapists stated that they did not feel adequately trained to assess bilingual children, with around 50 per cent stating that they did not assess these children for speech sound disorders. Those who did assess used informal assessments or standardised tests in English, which may not be appropriate for identifying the speech or language difficulties in these children. It is imperative, then, that appropriate training is also provided to speech and language therapists so that they feel confident in being able to assess and support children with autism who come from bilingual backgrounds and who may also have additional speech or language difficulties. As Dyches *et al.* (2007) and Wilder *et al.* (2004) argue, if therapists and teachers are to work effectively with children from multilingual backgrounds and their families, it is important that a better understanding of the impact of culture on the communication and learning of the children is developed among the workforce.

Social interaction

Developing social understanding and social skills is considered an important goal while working with children on the autism spectrum. The approaches that are often used are social skills groups or training through other means, such as video modelling or social scripts. As mentioned at the beginning of this chapter, social skills were an approach where ethnicity was mentioned in most of the studies included in Wong *et al.*'s (2014) evaluation. However, according to West *et al.* (2016), around 77 per cent of the participants in these studies were from a White background. The use of social scripts, which is another popular approach, did not provide any studies that included details about ethnicity. However, two other approaches – social narratives and video modelling – did include ethnicity, although the majority of these were single case studies conducted with White children. This leads to the same issue as in the area of communication – namely, how effective these approaches are for helping children from minority ethnic backgrounds. In the absence of any other alternative, care must be taken to ensure that these are adapted according to the needs of the child being worked with.

This is especially important, as the purpose of developing social skills is to enable an individual to be able to function within their community. For children with autism from different cultures, this means being able to function in more than one community or one set of norms. As has been explored in Chapter 2, there are differences in what different cultures consider appropriate social behaviours. In addition to the social behaviours that are specific to autism, there are also suggestions that there may be differences in some of the general social behaviours expected within an education setting. For example, Lee (2011) suggests that Asian American children may not participate within classroom discussions because within their culture it is considered rude to challenge or question an older person. John Lian (1996) states that this might also be the case in some African communities where children are taught to be obedient and respectful, which may mean that in these cultures asking questions or answering back to one's parents or elders is considered rude behaviour, whereas by contrast, this is expected behaviour in most Western European countries and in North American educational contexts. If a child does not engage in such a manner, it is likely that the teachers will perceive this as lack of interest or, alternatively, as a sign of a withdrawn child who needs to be encouraged to develop self-confidence. There is then a potential for a clash of views when home and school have different expectations from the child.

Considering the differences between expected behaviour in a school setting and cultural behaviour, Boykin (1994) suggests that there are potentially nine learning characteristics of African American students that may not meet Western educational expectations. Some of these behaviours that are particularly relevant when working with students on the autism spectrum are as follows:

- *Spirituality:* Students who are religious or who have a faith are likely to consider any positive or negative achievements at school to be the result of divine intervention. Teachers who do not share similar beliefs may consider that the child is working with an external locus of control, and may find it hard to support the student. I have worked with some young people on the autism spectrum coming from various ethnic backgrounds who had a strong religious belief, and their reactions corresponded to Boykin's suggestion.

- *Harmony:* Due to the history of Black people in the USA, it is likely that students from an African background expect to be treated with respect, and are especially sensitive to verbal or non-verbal means of communication where they feel they are being belittled. Understanding this is important, as lack of cultural awareness here could lead to behaviours that would be considered challenging. Considering the cultural differences in non-verbal behaviour, it is also important to understand which behaviours the child considers as offensive.

- *Emotional expression:* Boykin suggests that Black students are likely to be impulsive in their feelings and also express these accordingly. The overt and unhindered way of emotional expression may not be considered polite within Western contexts. As teaching emotional understanding tends to be an area of focus for children and young people with autism, it is again important to understand this difference in the cultural acceptability of expressions.

- *Collectivist:* African American students prefer to work collaboratively with others. This could be considered as lack of independence in Western societies, where a more individualist approach is appreciated.

- *Kinaesthetic:* Black students are supposed to prefer moving around, and are therefore more likely to be kinaesthetic learners. If this is also true for students with autism, this would be contrary to the accepted worldview in autism that describes them as visual learners. This means that better evaluation of preferred learning style is required when working with students with autism from different ethnic groups. It is also likely that this desire to move could be misinterpreted as hyperactivity.

- *Orality:* Students from African American communities might prefer expressing orally and could engage in debates and discussion that may be considered as argumentative behaviour. This preference for learning orally is also contrary to the expected learning styles in children with autism. This emphasis on oral learning also poses specific challenges when working with children who have limited speech.

- *Focused on social time:* Boykin suggests that students from Black communities like to focus on activities and are not as focused on completing tasks within set timelines. This means that they may find test time schedules or assignment deadlines frustrating, and may not be interested in following these. This could, of course, be perceived as a lack of organisation skills. Since it is assumed that students with autism may find organising problematic because of their executive functioning difficulties, it should, again, be carefully considered whether the exhibited behaviour is due to cultural norms, or part of autism, or a combination of both.

Although Boykin claims that these are specific learning patterns found in African American students, from my own experience I feel that students from other ethnic backgrounds also share some of these, and some of the existing research suggests that this might be the case. For example, Asian, West African and Hawaiian communities have been cited as communities that value interdependence or collectivism (Greenfield 1994; Hackett and Hackett 1993; Nsamenang and Lamb 1994; Tharp 1994). In all these cultures the individual is encouraged to think about the family and the immediate community, and to take responsibility for them. Interdependent communities tend to put the emphasis on being obedient and respecting one's parents and elders (Tharp 1994). As discussed earlier, not understanding the relevance of these behaviours may lead to confusion and frustration for the student, teachers and the family. What the list above does is draw attention to the fact that what is considered as appropriate learning behaviour may vary across cultures, and this needs to be considered when developing any intervention programmes.

Along with these cultural factors there are also differences in terms of gender and sexual orientation when it comes to acceptable social behaviours. For example, in many cultures it is considered 'unmanly' for a boy to cry in public. Lee (2011) suggests that certain words, such as 'gorgeous' or 'fabulous', are considered to be more feminine expressions of appreciation than male. Similarly, topics of conversation such as fashion or cosmetics are considered to be more appropriate for girls to be engaged in than boys. This also applies to aspects of social behaviour such as giving positive comments. For example, while it would be considered good social behaviour for a girl to appreciate someone else's dress or hair, if a boy exhibits the same behaviour, this is considered as odd. When someone's behaviour doesn't conform to the expected gender stereotype, society considers that the person is homosexual – for example, a girl discussing the merits of motorbikes. As each ethnic group has its own set of gender stereotypes for expected social behaviour, it is important that when teaching social skills attention is paid to the choice of vocabulary and topics as well as explaining the expected social behaviour.

The first step for developing social interaction skills is to understand what the expected social norms of the community are to which the child belongs. This then helps in developing social interaction goals that are appropriate for the child's specific culture. Based on the severity of autism and whether the child has any other associated conditions, it may have to be considered whether the child is likely to interact with people outside their family and community or not. This influences whether the child needs to be taught two sets of social behaviour – where the child is capable of learning different social expectations, two sets of social narratives or social behaviours need to be developed so that they can understand which would be considered appropriate in a given cultural context. Of course, for some social behaviours the child may need to learn only one set of behaviours – for example, the social expectations when visiting a family, where they are expected to follow the cultural norms. It is also possible that some families would like their children to learn only the social behaviours required within the majority community based on the acculturalisation of the family (see Perepa 2014), and this will need to be respected accordingly.

Most social skills training research studies do not provide sufficient information about how much of this adaptation of social skills and goals was undertaken while working with students from different ethnic groups. In a recent study, Chan *et al.* (2018) developed a culturally sensitive social skills training programme for Chinese students with autism in Hong Kong. Explaining the process of developing this, they suggest that everyday social contexts that were relevant for the students were identified and incorporated into the training. Culturally specific games were also used within the training and peer interaction sessions. Chan *et al.* report that the training thus developed has been successful in training 22 young people with autism in appropriate social behaviour. While the results are encouraging, and this is an example of developing indigenous intervention approaches, we need to remember that minority ethnic children living in different cultural contexts need two sets of social behaviour for successful integration, as explained above. I think that with increasing multicultural societies, understanding these different expectations is not only beneficial for the child from a minority ethnic community, but also for others in the group, because this will help them all to develop their cultural competence.

When a teacher or a therapist does not share the same cultural background, it can be harder to understand these differences in cultural expectations of social behaviour. While parents are a useful source of information in this area, we should be aware of the generational variance in social behaviour in order to avoid teaching the child social skills that are not age-appropriate. Involving siblings or other children from the same ethnic background would help in identifying goals that are also age-appropriate. Role-play or video modelling can be useful tools to show the students with autism the expected social norms for different age groups and therefore the expected behaviours. Although the current approaches used to teach social interaction skills do not provide evidence of their applicability in different ethnic groups, I think that some of these can be adapted for use with children from different ethnic groups. What is required is that specific attention is paid to the actual content of what the student is being taught.

Play skills

Play is considered to be an important part of a child's development because of its contribution towards language development, imaginative thinking and building social relationships, and a number of approaches in the field of autism focus on developing play skills or building relationships. Some assumptions are made about the universality of play when this happens. As discussed in Chapter 2, there seems to be variability in the type of play that children from different ethnic groups engage in as well as the objects that they use. This needs to be considered when focusing on developing play skills in children or engaging parents in such interventions. Just as with social skills, it is important to develop a good understanding of what are considered to be typical play skills in a given culture.

As play is often based on materials, it is important that the resources available in the setting are representative of the cultural backgrounds of the children. This could be in terms of toys, but also in terms of role-play material, music and any books that are used within the setting. Consideration should be given in selecting play partners for the intervention. Most approaches related to autism assume parents to be engaging in play, especially in early childhood. Lancy (2007) argues that there are differences in who are considered as ideal play partners in various cultures. In some cultures it is considered unusual for parents to engage in play with their children, and it would be considered especially rare for a stranger, such as a therapist, to play with the child. Where parents do engage, their expectation of appropriate play may differ from that of the professional involved. For example, Farver and Howes (1993) suggest that while it is common for White American mothers to engage in symbolic and pretend play with their children, mothers of children from a Mexican American background are more likely to engage in dyadic play, which almost seems like completing an activity rather than play to professionals who are unfamiliar with the cultural context. Along with differences in cultural norms, families may also find it hard to implement some intervention programmes because their family circumstances are not conducive to engaging in play activities (Mbise and Kysela 1990). It is important, therefore, when play-based interventions are selected, that sufficient attention is provided to the family expectations of play and how they would like to be involved in such activities. It may be more appropriate to work with siblings and use more integrated play strategies with some families than expecting parents to be the facilitators.

Collaborative working with families

While defining evidence-based practice, Aveyard and Sharp (2009) state that, along with having a clear rationale for using a specific approach that is based on research evidence and personal judgements, it is important to know clients' preferences. As most children do not have the legal right to provide their preference, it is important to work in partnership with their parents while deciding educational and therapeutic targets or strategies. In many countries such as the USA and UK and some provinces in Canada and Australia, there is a legal requirement for working in partnership with parents whose children have a special educational need such as autism.

Frameworks for parent–professional collaboration

Although there is increasing emphasis on collaborative working, the exact nature of the parent and professional relationship is often not well defined. In one of the few works that tries to provide a framework, Dale (1996) suggests five models of parent–professional involvement: expert, transplant, consumer, empowerment and negotiating. She explains that the expert model is where the role of the parent is primarily to seek guidance from the professional, who, being an expert in their field, is able to assess the child and provide appropriate interventions and targets. The parents' role is to provide the professional with the appropriate background information, such as the case history. In the transplant model the professional is still in charge of all clinical decisions, but they also provide guidance to the parents on how to follow up the suggested activities within the home setting. This is a familiar model of working with parents in a number of autism approaches such as TEACCH (Teaching, Expanding, Appreciating, Collaborating and Cooperating, and Holistic), and is often followed by speech and language therapists. In the consumer model the parents are the consumers who buy the required services, such as the speech and language therapy or occupational therapy. It is possible that in this model the parents may want the professionals to provide required information as well as strategies for working with their child. Some parents who are using Applied Behaviour Analysis (ABA) or the Options approach could be using this model to manage services for their child with autism. The empowerment model recognises that each family will be at a different stage in their readiness for working with professionals, and part of the professional's role is to empower the parents in this process. The negotiating model acknowledges that the parents and professionals may have different priorities and skills, so intervention for the child has to be negotiated by both parties. It accepts that the professional may have a better overview of the condition and the appropriate therapy or intervention strategy, but that the parent is the expert when it comes to their own child.

Looking at these different models of collaborative working, it is important to consider that each professional might prefer a specific way of working based on their training as well as personal preference. Similarly, parents may also have different expectations from professionals based on their personal preferences, cultural expectations and the family's personal situation. For example, Brice (2002) suggests that in Hispanic culture it is believed that the professional knows the best course of intervention for the child. It is expected that the family is respectful to the professionals as the experts. In such a situation, families may feel uncomfortable if they are expected to take a different role. These cultural differences between the role of the teacher or therapist and the parent have to be considered when working collaboratively with parents. However, it is important not to generalise experiences with one family from a specific cultural group to all the families from that community. In fact, Estrada and Deris (2014) report from their work with Hispanic parents that participants in their research were eager to discuss options with professionals, and felt that the professionals do not always know the appropriate way to work with their child with autism. Therefore, families coming from the same ethnic background could have different expectations from the professionals based on a range of reasons such as education, social status and acculturation.

Personal bias

It is important for the education professionals to be aware of their own bias and prejudice. For example, in the same study mentioned above, Estrada and Deris (2014) report that parents were often frustrated when working with the schools. The parents felt that the education professionals did not take their views and concerns seriously, and that they were treated as if they were a hindrance in the process.

They felt that the preconceived notions of the professionals about Hispanic parents might have influenced how the professionals treated the parents. Harry (2008) comments that when this is the case it will impact on whether or not the teachers and other professionals are willing to engage with the family, understand their perspective and include these in their planning of the provision. She further argues that some of the reasons for cross-cultural misunderstandings are because of the assumptions of family deficits, and being unaware of the logistical help that the family will require to participate in meetings or to follow the suggested strategies at home. I was aware of the importance of practical considerations when working with a single-parent family where we were using PECS successfully in the school setting. My colleagues very enthusiastically suggested to the mother that she should aim to have at least 50 exchanges every day with her child to help her make better progress. This mother had two other children and worked full time at a retail shop. My colleagues did not realise that while the suggested intervention was appropriate for the child, this was impractical within the family setting as the mother did not have any other adults to help her in the initial stages of PECS, nor the time to sabotage situations to create communication opportunities. Being realistic in what is expected from the family and looking at the family as a unit, when developing goals or suggesting strategies, would avoid such scenarios.

Bias about a culture or nationality is not limited to the parents but also affects the child, and it is important to be aware of this and to take active measures to overcome it. Based on their research on the correlation between the differences in the ethnicity of the student and the teacher, Neal *et al.* (2003) argue that where there is a difference, it is likely that the teachers may misinterpret the culture-specific behaviour of the child and that this could then lead to special education referrals. They found that where the teacher and the student shared the same ethnicity, it was less likely that these children would be referred to special education services. Serwatka, Deering and Grants (1995) lead this argument further by stating that the ethnicity of the teacher may have an impact for the outcomes achieved by a child with special educational needs from a minority ethnic community. Following a similar argument, Artiles, Trent and Palmer (2004) suggest that students from minority ethnic communities are more likely to be placed in restrictive settings because of bias, discrimination and systematic deficiencies in the US state education system. It is almost impossible to find teachers who will match the ethnicity of every student when working in multicultural societies. What is more realistic is to encourage the teachers and other professionals to be aware of their own personal bias and to challenge their perceptions. This means being reflective and regularly evaluating the decisions being made. As is acknowledged in the field of education, teachers' expectations have a significant impact on the students' outcomes, and therefore having high expectations from all children, irrespective of their ethnicity or disability, is important to provide optimum opportunities for all children.

Collaboration with parents

Professionals and parents sometimes disagree when considering support and interventions for children with autism, and there are several reasons for this. These could be based on how the parents and professionals view the development of the child, what they consider as appropriate goals for the child, and how they think these could be taught or realised. As has been explored in previous chapters, the concept of disability may be different in various cultural groups, which might impact on what the family considers as appropriate skills for their child to learn and what they consider their role as parents. For example, Mirza *et al.* (2009) report the views of Pakistani parents in their research where the parents considered having a child with disabilities as God's wish and they did not want to engage in any interventions. If fact, they felt that it was their role to look after their child's basic needs such as feeding, bathing and cleaning them. It is likely that if a family has such perceptions they may not be willing to teach their child self-help skills because they see it as their duty to look after such needs. Bevan-Brown (2004) suggests that a similar view is also held in the Māori community, where they consider it the duty of the community to look after individuals who are unable to look after themselves. This may be contrary to the expectations within a school setting where there is an emphasis on developing self-help skills and these are included in the targets for the child.

Differences in expected milestones for different ages may also have a similar effect. For example, Pachter and Dworkin (1997) and Schulze *et al.* (2002) suggest that Latino mothers expect their children to reach some of the milestones related to independence and social-emotional development at a later age than that considered normal by Western standards. If these areas become a focus for intervention, the parents may feel that the set targets are age-inappropriate for their child and may be disinclined to follow up the suggested intervention at home. Parents in Jegatheesan *et al.*'s (2010b) research also found it frustrating when the professionals were focusing on the limitations of their child, rather than accepting what they, the parents, considered to be the manifestation of God's will. Although these parents may not challenge the professionals because of the cultural expectations of giving respect to a professional, they may still not follow the intervention as they consider it to be inappropriate.

Religion could also play an important role in what the family considers as priorities for their child to learn. For example, Shaked (2005) reports that one of the main concerns for the ultra-Orthodox Jewish parents who took part in this research was whether their child with autism would be able to follow the Jewish rituals and rites, and if they would be able to engage in reading and discussing Jewish texts. As religion plays such a significant role for the cultural identity and social inclusion of these children, appropriate targets may need to focus on how these skills can be developed rather than trying to teach generic social skills or literacy in English. Unfortunately, the professionals may interpret these differing views as parents being in denial of the child's condition (Rogers-Adkinson *et al.* 2003) or not having realistic expectations from them. Asking the questions below could provide an opportunity to have an open discussion about parental expectations.

QUESTIONS FOR INITIAL DISCUSSION WITH PARENTS

1. What did you call your child's problem before it was diagnosed?

2. What do you think caused it?

3. What do you think autism does? How does it work?

4. How severe is it? Will it have a short or long course?

5. What are the chief problems your child's autism has caused?

6. What do you fear most about it?

7. What would you like your child to learn?

8. What kind of treatment do you think your child should receive?

9. What do you expect from this treatment?

10. What are your current priorities for your family?

11. What sources of support do you have?

(Adapted from Levy *et al.*'s (2003) questions)

Even when the targets are agreed, views may well differ as to how these can be developed. For example, it is possible that some families might feel that it is the professional's job to teach their child and not the parent's (Rodriguez and Olswang 2003). Or they may feel that the approach being used by the teacher or the therapist is not conducive for learning. For example, some parents from an Asian background may expect the intervention to be more structured and systematic than having a more child-centred approach. These expectations are often based on what they consider as good practice based on their own experience. Kim *et al.* (2011) report from their study that in South Korea the school system is highly structured and places a lot of emphasis on following rules and achieving academic success, with less emphasis on social activities. They suggest that this means that more able students with autism are capable of meeting the societal expectations and academic achievements. Parents who have seen children similar to their own thrive in a more structured environment are justified in considering that this would be a more appropriate way of teaching and learning than focusing on developing their child's social interaction skills, and that perhaps it is the educational system in the West that is disabling their child.

It is important in such instances to explain clearly to the parents why specific ways of teaching are being used with their child and the underlying philosophy. During these discussions it is important to involve all the family members who are likely to influence the childrearing approaches within that family. This means that the parent consultation meetings may have to be broadened to include whomever the family considers as important in such discussions. It is unlikely that there will be perfect agreement among all the family members and the professionals, and some level of flexibility or negotiation will also be required from the professionals. During my work with families from minority ethnic communities I also found that it is important to not make assumptions about the family's understanding of the educational procedures or their own role in the meeting. Cross-checking with the family that they actually understand the purpose of the meeting and the implications of the decisions is important. A family I was working with fought with the local authority to get their child into a special school. On the first day of the new term I received a phone call from the mother saying that the new school was one for 'disabled children'. It seems that this mother did not realise that when we use the term 'special school' in the UK we mean a school that educates children with disabilities. She interpreted the term 'special' as a better school! If we had spent time explaining the terminology, this misunderstanding could have been avoided, and the time spent in the following months in finding an alternative school for the child could have also been saved.

Previous experience of the education system and access to services will also have an impact on how satisfied the parents are with the education of their child and the provided services. For example, if the family came from a country that had limited access to schools for children with special educational needs, or did not have any legal rights for education, such a family is more likely to be satisfied with what is being provided than a family that is familiar with these systems. Communities that have historically suffered discrimination, such as the African American community in the USA, may have a different view of the provided services, and this may be reflected in their satisfaction levels. It should also be considered that a family stating that they are satisfied with the provision does not necessarily mean that this is the case, since it is possible that they are doing this because of the cultural expectation of deference to authority. Again, having open discussions to understand the family perceptions and not taking the criticism directly is important for any fruitful conversations.

Some families may find the formality of the meeting in an office too daunting. Spending time having a social conversation and providing a more relaxed room set-up can help in settling such families. For others, it might be preferable to have a home visit where discussions could take place within their familiar surroundings. This also means that a wider range of family members could participate in these discussions. Having first-hand experience of the context in which the child lives will also help the professionals in suggesting goals and strategies that are perhaps more realistic for their context.

The key message from this chapter is that it is important to be open and aware of the cultural bias of various approaches used in the field of autism and within educational settings. To provide culturally sensitive services it is important to be open to new sources of information, challenge our own preconceived notions, and be flexible in how we approach children with autism and their families.

A MOMENT TO PAUSE

— Have a chat with a colleague who comes from a different cultural background to understand how they perceive some of the procedures followed within your setting regarding behaviour management, organising meetings or working with families. Compare their views with your own.

— Watch a film from a different country to observe the social and communication styles being used. Consider how these compare with what would be considered appropriate in your own culture. What would be the implications for a student with autism who you may be supporting from such a cultural group?

Chapter 5

LIFE BEYOND
—— EDUCATION ——

Changes in the expectations of parents and children are a common occurrence of any family cycle as the children grow up and start establishing their own identity. This process can be intensified in families from minority ethnic communities due to the acculturation process. Berry *et al.* (1999) differentiate between enculturation and acculturation, defining enculturation as being surrounded by one's own culture, where learning often takes place without specific teaching. Acculturation, on the other hand, refers to cultural and psychological changes that are a result of contact with people belonging to different cultures and exhibiting different behaviours from one's own. An individual with autism born to minority ethnic parents could be going through an enculturation as well as acculturation process at the same time, where they will be learning the expected behaviours of their own culture and also realising that these are not shared by others in the wider community and therefore need adapting.

Joe (1994) states that during the process of acculturation a person will accept the means, tools and technology of the majority culture while still retaining their own values.

Berry (1980) refutes the idea that this is a seamless process, and suggests that acculturation be viewed as a multilinear phenomenon. The views of members of a group can differ on the basis of the time and manner in which the group has incorporated itself into a particular society. Harry (1992) says that the process of acculturation may also differ on the basis of education and social class, with higher social class and educated people finding it easier to acculturate. This means that the acculturation of families from the same ethnic group may vary for a range of reasons.

It is assumed that acculturation of a community increases with each generation. Mink (1997) rejects this idea, and states that this should not be considered a universal theory. An explanation for these differences of opinion is related to the migration history of a community or a family. Ogbu (1994) states that there are two types of minorities in the USA – voluntary and involuntary – based on their immigration process. His distinction is that voluntary minorities chose to come to the USA for a better life, whereas involuntary groups were incorporated into US society against their will (such as African Americans who had been brought over as slaves). This difference of origin is reflected in perceptions about the majority community. Ogbu suggests that voluntary minorities do not see the cultural frame of the dominant group as oppositional to their own, and try to acculturate into the society. Involuntary groups, on the other hand, develop and use secondary cultural differences for maintaining boundaries from the majority culture. They have no desire to overcome cultural and language differences, and peer pressure prevents members from the community from 'acting white'. This could have significant implications when teaching social skills to young people.

The difference between voluntary and involuntary communities is not as clear in other countries where the use of slaves was not as acceptable or as institutionalised. Economic immigrants coming to the UK or elsewhere in the Western world may be considered as voluntary minorities, as refugees, who had limited choice in selecting their country of residence, and second- or third-generation minorities may view themselves as involuntary minorities. Considering the impact of the dominant community's policies and practices, Ahmad *et al.* (1998) argue that concerns about the values and institutions of the wider society, as well as external hostility, reinforce strong and somewhat exclusive identities and proscribe the adoption of other cultural norms. This means that an individual's cultural identity could change at different points in their life based on the social and political factors in a given society. To explain why ethnic identity is becoming important for minority ethnic groups in the Western world, Banks (1986) suggests that it was because these communities felt that they could maintain their identity without shame on the basis of the egalitarian and democratic ideas in their host country. Groce (2005) says that another reason why cultural identity is becoming more important for immigrants now is the result of more opportunities for frequent travel to their country of origin, or having friends and family visit, both of which reinforce cultural identity, making acculturation less effective. With increasing use of the internet, it is also possible for individuals across the world to keep a closer link with their country of origin, by reading online newspapers, listening to radio programmes and watching films, all of which reinforce their cultural identity. Since access to some of these means vary based on age, it is also possible that different members of the same family could have their own individual cultural identity that may not be shared by all of the family. This could also be the case for different members of the same community. This highlights the importance of not generalising attitudes to people from a certain cultural background.

While some individuals with autism may not have the capacity or the means to build networks outside their immediate family, there will be others who are able to do so, and who may establish their own cultural identity and adopt behaviours that are in line with this. Where these are acceptable to the family's values, this may not cause any friction, but if this is not the case, it may lead to complications in providing adult services to people with autism. An increasing number of legislation and policies are being developed in various countries that also provide specific rights to individuals with autism. For example, in the UK the Mental Capacity Act (DCA 2005) assumes that every adult has the right to make decisions unless it has been proven not to be the case. This could be contrary to the expectations of some families, who feel that since the individual has a disability, they are not able to make any decisions. These differences in legal rights and individual opinions can be a source of stress when working with adults with autism from minority ethnic communities.

While there is much research on approaches to use with school-aged children with autism, this is not the case for post-education provision. In fact, there is very little research on approaches that are effective in working with young people and adults with autism, whether or not they are from diverse cultures. As a result, when we look at the list of evidence-based practice, there is little evidence of the efficacy of some of the strategies being used with adults with autism. There is even limited research exploring the views and issues for individuals coming from different cultures. Therefore, this brief chapter focuses mainly on the cultural implications when providing adult services rather than exploring how to support them. It explores some of the key themes that I think are relevant for adults and that are influenced by cultural issues, such as sex and relationships, the criminal justice system, employment and planning for adult care.

Sexuality and relationships

Sex and sexuality are an important part of human life, although this can be a complicated issue for someone with autism. There may be different opinions on what the various stakeholders in an individual think that a person is capable of and therefore able to prepare them for. Biologically there is no indication to suggest that sexual development is different in young people with autism compared to those without autism. Murphy and Elias' (2006) research suggests that young people with autism reach puberty around the same period as is expected from their peers. It is not the biological difference, but rather the nature of autism that can lead to different expectations. For example, it is often maintained that adults with autism lack the social and emotional understanding required to maintain a relationship, and that they may be socially naive. Differences in sensory perceptions may also make having intercourse difficult for some individuals. Cultural perceptions around disability, such as considering someone with a disability to be a preacher or acting as God's messenger, may impact on whether or not a community considers it appropriate for a young person with autism to have sex or to be part of an intimate relationship – these communities may feel that having sex would be contrary to the wishes of God for the individual. Parents may also choose to withdraw their children during their school years from sex education classes because of religious or cultural reasons, which may mean that some young people with autism from these communities will have no knowledge about this area, and consequently find it harder to understand their own physical and emotional needs.

Sex and female personal hygiene are often considered as intimate issues across most cultures, with the view that these should not be discussed with strangers or in public. If the young person with autism has limited social circles, this may result in having little understanding of what is expected from them. Some parents will provide a simplistic explanation because they feel uncomfortable about the topic or do not feel that their child is capable of understanding the complexities. I worked with a young Indian woman whose parents told her that when she had menstrual periods she was having an infection. This young girl then informed everyone that she was unwell and had an infection, to the dismay of the family. What the parents did not anticipate was that she would consider having an infection a major incident that needed to be reported to everyone. Some cultures have specific practices that need to be followed during this period, as it is associated with being impure. Certain families may want to follow these rituals and practices with a daughter who may or may not be able to understand these procedures, or may feel that such customs are outdated or unnecessary. Professionals involved with the individual will need to support the individual and their family accordingly.

Some adults with autism may not understand the social conventions about sexual acts or display of their body and may perhaps masturbate in public, touch others inappropriately or show their private body parts to others. This can cause embarrassment to people in most cultures, which might be increased in cultural groups where sexual behaviour is considered to be taboo. What is considered as appropriate touch or exhibition of intimacy could also vary based on culture. For example, it is considered normal for boys in the Middle East to hold each other's hand as friends, whereas such public display of affection between two members of the opposite sex would be considered as highly inappropriate. Conversely, in most Western societies, if two men are holding hands it would be considered that they were homosexuals, and public display of such affection between men and women would not cause any embarrassment. A young person or adult with autism needs to understand these different expectations and change their behaviours to avoid any misunderstandings.

There is a higher incidence of single-parent families in some of the African communities because of their cultural history (Miller 2005), which usually means that the young person with autism is living with their mother. This can cause particular difficulty if the young person is a male and the mother does not feel confident or comfortable teaching about masturbation or sexual hygiene. Not explaining the expected behaviour could place the individual in a vulnerable position. For example, I worked with an adult with autism who was not taught how to use public toilets. As a result, every time we went into the community and he needed to use the lavatory, he would remove his trousers as well as his underwear before using the urinal, much to the amusement and embarrassment of the other men in the toilet. Exposing himself in such a way could have been considered as deliberate exhibitionism, as well as making him vulnerable for sexual abuse. In fact, research suggests that children with developmental disabilities are twice as likely to be sexually abused compared to children without disabilities (Mansell, Sobsey and Moskal 1998). There is no reason to think that such incidents do not carry on into adulthood as well, when the individual is more likely to be alone or living independently. Therefore, teaching about appropriate sexual behaviour from a young age is important to safeguard people with autism, and if the family is unable to provide such knowledge, professionals will need to take this role.

Some adults with autism may want to have a partner or get married because this is what is expected as part of adulthood, without necessarily understanding the intricacies involved in such relationships. Research suggests that adults with autism are less likely to be married, with less than 15 per cent being in a long-term relationship or being married (Howlin and Moss 2012). However, this study does not indicate how many of these adults were from a minority ethnic background. It is likely that the idea of marriage may actually appeal to the cultural norms of some communities. For example, in their research into attitudes towards individuals with autism in the British Asian community, Dobson and Upadhyaya (2002) found that some members in this community thought that getting the person married would cure their autism. If such views are held in a community, even individuals with more severe autism could be taken through the process of marriage without their understanding its implications. It is important in these instances to provide support to the individual and their partner in order for them to understand the implications of marriage. On the other hand, some families may consider that their child with autism is not capable of understanding the consequences of physical intimacy, and therefore choose to sterilise the person. While local legislation about such a process is different across countries, the human rights of the young person also need to be protected. The role of professionals in such situations needs to be to act as an advocate for the individual and to discuss the issue with the family and help them teach the young person about sex and how to differentiate between desired and undesired touch.

There is a whole range of cultural and religious beliefs and attitudes around homosexuality – for example, some who accept this as a norm, others who feel that it is unnatural, or those who consider it a sin. While an increasing number of adults with autism say they are homosexual or that they do not believe in the binary concept of gender, sex education, where it exists, often doesn't cover homosexual relationships or the implications of being a transgender person. There is also limited support available from organisations that work with different sexual orientations when it comes to people with disabilities such as autism. This could mean that an individual with autism will need to negotiate this complex world of cultural and religious expectations while also coming to terms with and expressing who they are. There is an urgent need to prepare professionals who are able to provide such support to these individuals on the autism spectrum.

Criminal justice system

There is increasing interest in exploring the relation between criminal behaviour and autism, especially as a result of a number of cases reported in the media where this association is made. Research evidence for this seems to be more varied than would be assumed based on these media reports. For example, Hare *et al.* (1999) report the percentage of people with autism in secure hospitals in the UK to be around 1.6 per cent, which they consider is higher than expected rates. Similarly, Siponmaa *et al.* (2001) found in their research in Sweden that the incidence of autism in young offenders was as high as 15 per cent. However, studies conducted by Woodbury-Smith *et al.* (2006) in the UK and Mouridsen *et al.*'s (2008) research in Denmark suggest that the figures are much lower than these. It is hard to guess why there is this disparity. It could be that some individuals with autism are kept in secure units for longer periods, hence the higher incidence rates in the first reported studies. If this is the case, the location of where these studies are conducted must impact on the results. Not many of the studies related to offending behaviour and autism specifically report or detail the ethnic breakdown, so it is hard to provide concrete figures or to understand how much of an issue this is for adults with autism from different cultures. However, considering that there is a higher prevalence rate of people from some minority ethnic communities in prisons, it is likely that the figures related to individuals with autism could be similar.

The most common type of crimes that young people with autism are likely to engage in is violence (Woodbury-Smith *et al.* 2006) and arson (Siponmaa *et al.* 2001). It is understandable why this might be the case based on the difficulties in the areas of communication and social interaction, and the strong interests that some individuals with autism could have. Fascination with fire may lead to accidents that could be viewed as arson attacks. This link with special interest could also be the reason for the increasing reports of people with autism engaged in cyber-crime.

The socio-political scenario in the West makes individuals from certain ethnic and religious backgrounds particularly vulnerable to being identified as committing criminal offences. I was aware of a Sikh adult with autism who was frequently stopped and searched in London following the 2005 bombing, as police often mistook him for a Muslim because of his beard and headgear. While this individual was able to go through these situations without getting too anxious, it is easy to see how such situations may cause difficulty for some other people with autism. The physical proximity and sensory nature of a search can be difficult to bear for some adults, along with not understanding why they are being stopped. This confusion and unpleasantness may then trigger violent behaviour, which would only lead to further complications for the individual.

Some people with autism express a strong desire to be part of a community or a social circle. This can make them vulnerable to all kinds of bullying and abuse, where others will take advantage of their need for social groups and make them perform acts that they may not want to do, or where they may not understand the implications of their behaviour. It could also be easy to radicalise some individuals based on their religious beliefs, as places of worship or the internet may also provide an opportunity for socialisation that some people with autism seek. As implied at the beginning of this chapter, some second- and third-generation immigrants follow their religious and cultural norms with more zeal as part of their search for their identity. While understanding this need for cultural identity, it is still important to explain to them the dangers involved in being part of such groups. Part of the social skills training programmes need to focus on teaching individuals with autism to say 'no' when they do not want to be part of an activity. This is important for their safety in a number of situations.

Employment

Finding a job to gain independence is an aim that most people nurture. However, this may not be a reality for many young people with autism. For example, in a survey conducted by Bancroft *et al.* (2012), it was found that a third of the young people between the ages of 16 and 24 with autism reported that they were not in education, employment or training (NEET). If these young people do not have access to education or training, it makes it particularly hard for them to find any employment. It is no wonder, then, that Higgins (2009) reports that around 50 per cent of adults with autism over the age of 25 are dependent on their parents for their finances and are also living at home. Although both these reports are from the UK, the picture is not very positive when looking at the evidence for employment of individuals with autism across various countries. For example, a recent study conducted in Taiwan by Chen *et al.* (2017) also reports that around half of their participants were not in employment or education. Finding appropriate employment and being able to maintain it seems to be a challenge for many adults with autism.

When the situation is already difficult, cultural expectations about family structures can partly influence what the families aspire to for their family member with autism. For example, Brice (2002) suggests that in Hispanic communities a value is placed on the interdependent nature of their family structure. This means that children in this community are brought up not to pursue their personal goals or foster independence, but are encouraged to be part of a family and work towards the betterment of the family unit. In such situations the family may prefer the person with autism to do some household chores rather than go out to seek employment. As discussed above, the process of acculturation may be different for each family. This difference in perceptions can be seen in another study conducted with Hispanic parents (Estrada and Deris 2014), where it was found that the parents were keen for their children to be able to work when they grew up and were independent. The contrasting views are perhaps a reflection of the length of time some of these families had lived in the USA, which facilitated the process of acculturation and which then led to similar aspirations as in mainstream American society, or it could be the result of recruiting different sets of parents for both these studies. What it highlights again is the individual nature of families from a specific community, and that we should not stereotype an ethnic group based on one source of information.

Understanding cultural values is useful, however, to get an insight into how a community works and the potential priorities for that group. Expanding on the family values of Hispanic families in the USA, Calzada (2010) states that these families favour *familismo*, or a responsibility towards family that can be seen in the following five areas:

- A focus on shared finances where family members support each other in times of need.

- Shared living, where extended family such as parents, in-laws, siblings and cousins are all living together.

- Shared childrearing by all the adults in the family.

- Shared daily activities where family members spend time together when they are free.

- These shared principles would also mean that families support each other in migrating to the USA.

Some of these principles are probably also true for families coming from other minority ethnic groups. Having this view of shared responsibility may mean that they might not want an individual with autism to pursue paid work as long as they are able to successfully contribute to other areas of the family living. While elders in the family may have such a view, it is important to ascertain whether those with autism share this view. Some families may also have inhibitions about allowing their family member to work in what they consider menial jobs. This could include a number of vocational skills that some people with autism are traditionally trained for, such as office assistance, cooking or cleaning. This may make it hard for the person to be able to work and gain independence. The role of professionals in such situations has to be that of negotiator and facilitator to explain the wishes of the young person with autism, while also understanding the concerns and ideas of the family members.

Even when the family agrees to the person working, people from minority ethnic communities may need extra preparation for employment as their communication and interaction style may not be appropriate to seek employment due to cultural differences. Therefore, adults with autism not only face the challenges of lack of awareness about autism and negative stereotypes about the condition, but also the stereotypes and lack of understanding regarding their cultural behaviour. An employment support scheme working for such adults will need to train the colleagues and employer in cultural awareness as well as autism awareness.

Adult care

If most adults with autism are either living at home or in care situations, it is important to also train them in independent living skills so that they can be contributing members within their family, or if they are living independently, so that they are able to look after themselves. When training in daily living skills it is necessary to understand the cultural expectations that are related to these routine activities – for example, understanding the appropriate way to wash dishes or knowing whether people from a specific cultural group brush their teeth before breakfast or after. Similarly it is more appropriate for some people to include learning to cook some traditional food items. Understanding these subtleties is important in preparing these young people to successfully navigate their own culture and to be socially accepted members of their community.

On the whole, adult care tends to be set up with the understanding that families would prefer to access some sort of residential care. However, as studies show, most adults with autism are living with their families (Howlin and Moss 2012). There could be several reasons for this, and not all families will be pleased about the arrangement. In a comparative study of 108 White and Latino mothers who were co-residing with their child with autism, Magaña and Smith (2006) found that mothers coming from White American backgrounds were more distressed and had lower levels of mental wellbeing compared to Latino mothers.

Although both groups of mothers valued the opportunity for family cohesion, Latino mothers reported fewer negative aspects of such an arrangement. Magaña and Smith argue that there is a correlation between the level of satisfaction of the parents about living with their child and their emotional wellbeing. This difference in satisfaction levels could be a result of cultural expectations. As described above, cohabitation is an accepted part of Hispanic culture and so having a son or daughter at home might be less distressing for these mothers. This research shows that there is a need to support families from different ethnic backgrounds in a way that is based on their expectations for adulthood. Of course, what this research does not explore are the views of those with autism. More of a focus on understanding their needs and including these in planning services is required.

In another comparative study of the social participation of young people with autism in Taiwan and Australia, Chen *et al.* (2017) found that Taiwanese young people with autism had fewer opportunities for social interaction. They suggest that this could be a reflection of the cultural perceptions regarding people with disabilities where there is stigma attached to such conditions, which then restricts their opportunities for going out. What was also interesting was that females in both countries were more engaged in social interaction than males, again perhaps a reflection of the gender stereotypes held in most cultures that provide females with more opportunities for interaction. This study did not explore whether these young people were happy with the level of social participation that they were able to access. Due to the diversity of the spectrum, different individuals with autism may have specific expectations about being part of social groups and having opportunities for interaction. There is some evidence suggesting that there could be a potential link between the opportunities for social interaction and an individual's mental health. Therefore, it is important to understand how the individual feels about being at home or in a residential home that limits their opportunities for socialising, and to create opportunities for this to happen, if required.

Person-centred planning

All these discussions could be held as part of planning for the transition from children's services to adult services. Person-centred planning (PCP) is becoming common in adult services in various countries, although it may be called other names. The aim of PCP is to help individuals to plan for their future lives by exploring their aspirations and desires. Significant people in the individual's life are invited to these planning meetings to explore the sources of support that the individual has as well as offering an opportunity to explore other possible future options. PCPs have received some criticism as they are more often used to plan services for young people with severe autism than for more able young people with the condition, with some arguing that individuals with more severe communication difficulties and intellectual disabilities are more likely to receive services than those who have fewer difficulties in these areas. This could be related to the fact that in some countries, such as the UK, while there are established services for adults with intellectual disabilities, this is not always the case for individuals with a diagnosis of autism without intellectual disabilities. These differences are not always explained to the families, which could then lead to frustration.

In a study conducted with Latino parents, Estrada and Deris (2014) found that parents were frustrated as they had no knowledge about what options there were for their child's future. As adult services are not structured in the same way as education, they also felt out of control. The parents reported that they were not aware of their or their child's legal rights. This means that individuals with autism from minority ethnic communities and their families may not be able to contribute in a useful way because they do not have a clear idea of their rights and options. To facilitate a successful PCP meeting it is important that this information is provided in a clear and accessible way. As this book has been highlighting throughout, there is a divergence in cultural expectations, communication and interaction styles, and how different cultures express their emotions. These need to be accommodated to have a fruitful discussion. Similarly, it is likely that neither the adult with autism nor their family members have adequate literacy skills in English, so alternative ways of recording their thoughts and plans need to be considered. Callicott (2003) offers some useful guidelines on providing culturally sensitive PCPs. As every adult knows, our aspirations and future plans are not set in stone and are likely to change at different points of life. Therefore, PCPs should not be just a formality that happens at the point of transition; there should be opportunities for these discussions to take place at different points in the life of the person.

A MOMENT TO PAUSE

— How could you assess the importance of culture to the young person or the adult you are working with?

— What steps would you take to provide opportunities for engagement with their cultural or religious practices if these are important to the individual?

— Consider how you will support a young person or an adult when their views are different from those of their family members.

Final Word

We have come to the end of this book having explored various aspects related to ethnicity and autism. I have been at pains to point out that there is very little published research into this topic, and there is a great deal that we do not know about the interaction of culture with autism, and the implications of this for working with a person with autism or their family. This book makes a small attempt to bring some of these issues into the light. There is a need for genuine effort to understand how the differences associated with autism are understood and supported in various cultures. It is important not to assume that the way we address these in the West is necessarily the best or the only way. Every community develops concepts, services and good practice guidelines based on what works for them. A respectful way of working with individuals who do not come from the same cultural background is to understand which of these are still appropriate for these people. It should not be just a case of other cultures having to learn from us; there must be opportunities for learning from each other to allow every individual, whether they have a label of autism or not, to achieve the very best that they possibly can.

References

Adams, C. (2002) 'Practitioner review: The assessment of language pragmatics.' *Journal of Child Psychology and Psychiatry 43*, 973–987.

Ahmad, W., Darr, A., Jones, L. and Nisar, G. (1998) *Deafness and Ethnicity.* Bristol: Policy Press.

Al-Farsi, Y., Al-Sharbati, M.M., Al-Farsi, O.A., Al-Shafaee, M.S., Brooks, D.R. and Waly, M.I. (2011) 'Brief report: Prevalence of autistic spectrum disorders in the Sultanate of Oman.' *Journal of Autism and Developmental Disabilities 41*, 821–825.

Ametepee, L. and Chitiyo, M. (2009) 'What we know about autism in Africa: A brief research synthesis.' *Journal of the International Association of Special Education 10*, 11–13.

Angell, A. and Solomon, O. (2017) '"If I was a different ethnicity, would she treat me the same?" Latino parents' experiences obtaining autism services.' *Disability & Society 32*(8), 1142–1164.

Angell, A., Frank, G. and Solomon, O. (2016) 'Latino families' experiences with autism services: Disparities, capabilities, and occupational justice.' *OTJR: Occupation, Participation, Health 36*(4), 195–203.

APA (American Psychiatric Association) (1980) *Diagnostic and Statistical Manual of Mental Disorders* (3rd edn). Washington, DC: APA.

APA (1987) *Diagnostic and Statistical Manual of Mental Disorders* (3rd edn, text rev.). Washington, DC: APA.

APA (2013) *Diagnostic and Statistical Manual of Mental Disorders* (5th edn). Washington, DC: APA.

Artiles, A.J., Trent, S.C. and Palmer, J. (2004) 'Culturally Diverse Students in Special Education: Legacies and Prospects.' In J.A. Banks and C.M. Banks (eds) *Handbook of Research on Multicultural Education* (2nd edn) (pp.716–735). San Francisco, CA: Jossey-Bass.

Aveyard, H. and Sharp, P. (2009) *A Beginner's Guide to Evidence Based Practice in Health and Social Care Professions.* Maidenhead: Open University Press.

Ayers, A.J. (1979) *Sensory Integration and the Child*. Los Angeles, CA: Western Psychological Services.

Bachmann, C., Gerste, B. and Hoffmann, F. (2018) 'Diagnoses of autism spectrum disorders in Germany: Time trends in administrative prevalence and diagnostic stability.' *Autism 22*(3), 283–290.

Baio, J., Wiggins, L., Christensen, D.L., Maenner, M.J., *et al.* (2018) 'Prevalence of autism spectrum disorder among children aged 8 years – Autism and Developmental Disabilities Monitoring Network, 11 sites, United States, 2014.' *Morbidity and Mortality Weekly Report (MMWR) Surveillance Summaries 67*(6), 1–23. doi: http://dx.doi.org/10.15585/mmwr.ss6706a1

Baird, G., Simonoff, E., Pickles, A., Chandler, S., *et al.* (2006) 'Prevalence of disorders of the autistic spectrum in a population cohort of children in South Thames: The Special Needs and Autism Project.' *Lancet 368*, 210–215.

Bancroft, K., Batten, A., Lambert, S. and Maddens, T. (2012) *The Way We Are: Autism in 2012*. London: The National Autistic Society.

Banks, J.A. (1986) 'Multicultural Education: Development, Paradigms and Goals.' In J.A. Banks and J. Lynch (eds) *Multicultural Education in Western Societies* (pp.2–28). Eastbourne: Holt, Rinehart & Winston.

Barnevik-Olsson, M., Gillberg, C. and Fernell, E. (2008) 'Prevalence of autism in children born to Somali parents living in Sweden: A brief report.' *Developmental Medicine and Child Neurology 50*, 598–601.

Baron-Cohen, S., Leslie, A.M. and Frith, U. (1985) 'Does the autistic child have a "theory of mind"?' *Cognition 21*, 37–46.

Baron-Cohen, S., Scott, F.J., Allison, C., Williams, J., *et al.* (2009) 'Prevalence of autism-spectrum conditions: UK school-based population study.' *British Journal of Psychiatry 194*, 500–509.

Baron-Cohen, S., Wheelwright, S., Skinner, R., Martin, J. and Clubley, E. (2001) 'The Autism Spectrum Quotient (AQ): Evidence from Asperger syndrome/high functioning autism, males and females, scientists and mathematicians.' *Journal of Autism and Developmental Disorders 31*, 5–17.

Begeer, S., Bouk, S.E., Boussaid, W., Terwogt, M.M. and Koot, H.M. (2009) 'Under diagnosis and referral bias of autism in ethnic minorities.' *Journal of Autism and Developmental Disorders 39*, 142–148.

Bennett, C. (1986) *Comprehensive Multicultural Education*. Boston, MA: Allyn & Bacon.

Berry, J.W. (1980) 'Acculturation as Varieties of Adaptation.' In A. Padilla (ed.) *Acculturation: Theory, Models and Some New Findings* (pp.9–25). Boulder, CO: Westview.

Berry, J.W. (1999) 'On the Unity of the Field of Culture and Psychology.' In J. Adamopoulos and U. Kashima (eds) *Social Psychology and Cultural Context* (Chapter 1). London: Sage Publications.

Berry, J.W. and Kim, U. (1993) 'The Way Ahead – From Indigenous Psychologies to a Universal Psychology.' In U. Kim and J.W. Berry (eds) *Indigenous Psychologies* (pp.277–280). Newbury Park, CA: Sage Publications.

Berry, J.W., Poortinga, Y.H., Segall, M.H. and Dasen, P.R. (1999) *Cross-cultural Psychology.* Cambridge: Cambridge University Press.

Bevan-Brown, J. (2004) *Māori Perspectives of Autistic Spectrum Disorder.* Wellington: Ministry of Education.

Bishop, S.L., Richler, J., Cain, A.C. and Lord, C. (2007) 'Predictors of perceived negative impact in mothers of children with autism spectrum disorder.' *American Journal of Mental Retardation 112*, 450–461.

Blais, C., Jack, R.E., Scheepers, C., Fiset, D. and Caldara, R. (2008) 'Culture shapes how we look at faces.' *PLoS One 3*(8), 1–8.

Boykin, A.W. (1994) 'Afrocultural Expression and Its Implications for Schooling.' In E.R. Hollins, J.E. King and W.C. Hayman (eds) *Teaching Diverse Populations: Formulating a Knowledge Base* (pp.243–273). Albany, NY: State University of New York Press.

Brice, A. (2002) *The Hispanic Child: Speech, Language, Culture and Education.* Boston, MA: Allyn & Bacon.

Broder-Fingert, S., Shui, A., Pulcini, C., Kurowski, D. and Perrin, J. (2013) 'Racial and ethnic differences in subspecialty service use by children with autism.' *Pediatrics 132*(1), 94–100.

Callicott, K. (2003) 'Culturally sensitive collaboration with person-centred planning.' *Focus on Autism and Other Developmental Disabilities 18*(1), 60–68.

Calzada, E. (2010) 'Bringing culture into parent training with Latinos.' *Cognitive and Behavioral Practice 17*(2), 167–175.

Cappiello, M.M. and Gahagan, S. (2009) 'Early child development and developmental delay in indigenous communities.' *Pediatric Clinics of North America 56*, 1501–1517.

Carter, J.A., Lees, J.A., Muria, G.M., Gona, J., Neville, B.G.R. and Newton, C.R.J.C. (2005) 'Issues in the development of cross-cultural assessments of speech and language for children.' *International Journal of Language and Communication Disorders 40*, 385–401.

CDC (Centers for Disease Control and Prevention) (2014) 'Prevalence of autism spectrum disorders among children aged 8 years – Autism and Developmental Disabilities Monitoring Network, 11 sites, United States, 2010.' *Morbidity and Mortality Weekly Report 63*(2), 1–21.

Chaidez, V., Hansen, R.L. and Hertz-Picciotto, I. (2012) 'Autism spectrum disorders in Hispanics and non-Hispanics.' *Autism: The International Journal of Research and Practice 16*(4), 381–397.

Chan, R., Leung, C., Yiu Ng, D. and Yau, S. (2018) 'Validating a culturally-sensitive social competence training programme for adolescents with ASD in a Chinese context: An initial investigation.' *Journal of Autism and Developmental Disorders 48*, 450–460.

Chan, S. (1986) 'Parents of Exceptional Asian Children.' In M.K. Kitano and P.C. Chin (eds) *Exceptional Asian Children and Youth* (pp.36–53). Arlington, VA: Council for Exceptional Children.

Chen, Y., Bundy, A., Cordier, R., Chien, Y. and Einfeld, S. (2017) 'A cross-cultural exploration of the everyday social participation of individuals with autism spectrum disorders in Australia and Taiwan: An experience sampling study.' *Autism 21*(2), 231–241.

Chua, H.F., Boland, J.E. and Nisbett, R.E. (2005) 'Cultural variation in eye movements during scene perception.' *Proceedings of the National Academy of Sciences of the United States of America 102*(35), 12629–12633.

Cimpric, A. (2010) *Children Accused of Witchcraft: An Anthropological Study of Contemporary Practices in Africa.* Dakar: UNICEF WCARO. Accessed on 14 September 2018 at www.unicef.org/wcaro/english/wcaro_children-accused-of-witchcraft-in-Africa.pdf

Collett, P. (1971) 'Training Englishmen in the non-verbal behaviour of Arabs.' *International Journal of Psychology 6*(3), 209–215.

Connors, J. and Donnellan, A. (1993) 'Citizenship and culture: The role of disabled people in Navajo society.' *Disability & Society 8*(3), 265–280.

Cote, L. and Bornstein, M. (2000) 'Social and didactic parenting behaviors and beliefs among Japanese American and South American mothers of infants.' *Infancy 1*, 363–374.

Creak, M. (1964) 'Schizophrenic syndrome in childhood: Future progress report of a working party.' *Developmental Medicine and Child Neurology 6*, 530–535.

Croen, L., Grether, J. and Selvin, S. (2002) 'Descriptive epidemiology of autism in a California population: Who is at risk?' *Journal of Autism and Developmental Disorders 32*, 217–224.

Cuccaro, M., Wright, H., Rownd, C., Abramson, R., Waller, J. and Fender, D. (1996) 'Brief report. Professional perceptions of children with developmental difficulties: The influence of race and socioeconomic status.' *Journal of Autism and Developmental Disorders 26*(4), 461–469.

Cummins, J. (2000) *Language, Power and Pedagogy: Bilingual Children in the Crossfire.* Clevedon: Multilingual Matters.

Dale, N. (1996) *Working with Families of Children with Special Needs.* London: Routledge.

Daley, T. (2004) 'From symptom recognition to diagnosis: Children with autism in urban India.' *Social Science & Medicine 58*, 1323–1335.

DCA (Department for Constitutional Affairs) (2005) *Mental Capacity Act*. London: The Stationery Office.

Dilworth-Anderson, P., Brummett, B.H., Goodwin, P., Williams, S.W., Williams, R.B. and Siegler, I.C. (2005) 'Effect of race on cultural justifications for caregiving.' *Journal of Gerontology: Social Sciences 60*, S257–S262.

Dobson, S. and Upadhyaya, S. (2002) 'Concepts of autism in Asian communities in Bradford, UK.' *Good Autism Practice 3*(2), 43–51.

Duranti, A. and Ochs, E. (1996) 'Use and Construction of Genitive Constructions in Samoan.' In D. Slobin, J. Gerdhardt, A. Kyratzis and G. Jiansheng (eds) *Social Interaction, Social Context and Language: Essays in Honour of Susan Ervin Tripp* (pp.175–190). Mahwah, NJ: Lawrence Erlbaum Associates.

Dyches, T., Wilder, L., Algozzine, B. and Obiakor, F. (2007) 'Working with Multicultural Learners with Autism.' In F.E. Obiakor (ed.) *Multicultural Special Education: Culturally Responsive Teaching* (Chapter 9). Upper Saddle River, NJ: Pearson.

Dyches, T., Wilder, L., Sudweeks, R., Obiakor, F. and Algozzine, B. (2004) 'Multicultural issues in autism.' *Journal of Autism and Developmental Disorders 34*(2), 211–222.

Edwards, C.P. (2000) 'Children's play in cross-cultural perspective: A new look at the six cultures study.' *Cross-Cultural Research 34*, 318–338.

El Bouk, S., Boussaid, W., Meerum Terwogt, M. and Koot, H. (2009) 'Under-diagnosis and referral bias of autism in ethnic minorities.' *Journal of Autism and Developmental Disorders 39*(1), 142–148.

Elfenbein, H.A. (2013) 'Nonverbal dialects and accents in facial expressions of emotion.' *Emotion Review 5*(1), 90–96.

Elfenbein, H.A., Beaupré, M., Lévesque, M. and Hess, U. (2007) 'Toward a dialect theory: Cultural differences in the expression and recognition of posed facial expressions.' *Emotion 7*(1), 131.

Ember, C.R. and Cunnar, C.M. (2015) 'Children's play and work: The relevance of cross-cultural ethnographic research for archaeologists.' *Childhood in the Past 8*(2), 87–103.

Estrada, L. and Deris, A. (2014) 'A phenomenological examination of the influence of culture on treating and caring for Hispanic children with autism.' *International Journal of Special Education 29*(3), 4–15.

Farmer, E., Burns, B., Angold, A. and Costello, E. (1997) 'Impact of children's mental health problems on families: Relationships with service use.' *Journal of Emotional and Behavioral Disorders 5*, 230–238.

Farver, J.M. and Howes, C. (1993) 'Cultural differences in American and Mexican mother–child pretend play.' *Merrill-Palmer Quarterly 39*, 344–358.

Farver, J.M. and Lee-Shin, Y. (1997) 'Social pretend play in Korean and Anglo-American preschoolers.' *Child Development 68*, 536–544.

Farver, J.M. and Lee-Shin, Y. (2000) 'Acculturation and Korean-American children's social and play behaviour.' *Social Development 9*(3), 316–336.

Fombonne, E. (2007) 'Epidemiological Surveys of Prevalence Developmental Disorders.' In F. Volkmar (ed.) *Autism and Pervasive Developmental Disorders* (2nd edn) (pp.33–69). New York: Cambridge.

Freeth, M., Sheppard, E., Ramachandran, R. and Milne, E. (2013) 'A cross-cultural comparison of autistic traits in the UK, India and Malaysia.' *Journal of Autism and Developmental Disabilities 43*, 2569–2583.

Frith, U. (1989) *Autism: Explaining the Enigma.* Oxford: Blackwell.

Frith, U. (1991) 'Autistic Psychopathy in Childhood by Hans Asperger.' In U. Frith (ed.) *Autism and Asperger Syndrome* (pp.37–92). Cambridge: Cambridge University Press.

Fugita, S., Wexley, K. and Hillery, J. (1974) 'Black–White differences in nonverbal behavior in an interview setting.' *Journal of Applied Social Psychology 4*(4), 343–350.

Gabel, S. (2004) 'South Asian Indian cultural orientations toward mental retardation.' *Mental Retardation 42*, 12–25.

Gillberg, C., Steffenberg, S., Borjesson, B. and Anderson, L. (1987) 'Infantile autism in children of immigrant parents: A population-based study from Goteborg, Sweden.' *British Journal of Psychiatry 150*, 856–858.

Gillberg, C., Steffenberg, S. and Schaumann, H. (1991) 'Is autism more common now than ten years ago?' *British Journal of Psychiatry 158*, 403–409.

Gona, J., Newton, C., Rimba, K., Mapenzi, R., *et al.* (2015) 'Parents' and professionals' perceptions on causes and treatment options for autism spectrum disorders (ASD) in a multicultural context on the Kenyan coast.' *PLoS One 10*(8), e0132729. doi: 10.1371/journal.pone.0132729

Goodman, R. and Richards, H. (1995) 'Child and adolescent psychiatric presentations of second-generation Afro-Caribbeans in Britain.' *British Journal of Psychiatry 167*, 362–369.

Greenfield, P.M. (1994) 'Independence and Interdependence as Developmental Scripts: Implications for Theory, Research, and Practice.' In P. Greenfield and R. Cocking (eds) *Cross-cultural Roots of Minority Child Development* (pp.1–37). Mahwah, NJ: Lawrence Erlbaum Associates.

Grinker, R.R. (2007) *Unstrange Minds: Remapping the World of Autism.* New York: Basic Books.

Groce, N. (2005) 'Immigrants, Disability, and Rehabilitation.' In J.H. Stone (ed.) *Culture and Disability* (Chapter 1). Los Angeles, CA: Sage Publications.

Groce, N. and Zola, I. (1993) 'Multiculturalism, chronic illness, and disability.' *Paediatrics 91*(5), 1048–1055.

Gutierrez-Clellen, V. (1999) 'Language choice in intervention with bilingual children.' *American Journal of Speech-Language Pathology 8*(4), 291–302.

Hackett, L. and Hackett, R. (1993) 'Parental ideas of normal and deviant child behaviour – A comparison of two ethnic groups.' *British Journal of Psychiatry 162*, 353–357.

Haight, W., Wang, X., Fung, H., Williams, K. and Mintz, J. (1999) 'Universal, developmental, and variable aspects of young children's play: A cross-cultural comparison of pretending at home.' *Child Development 70*, 1477–1488.

Hare, D., Gould, J., Mills, R. and Wing, L. (1999) *A Preliminary Study of Individuals with Autistic Spectrum Disorders in Three Special Hospitals in England*. London: The National Autistic Society.

Harper, J. and Williams, S. (1976) 'Infantile autism: The incidence of national groups in a New South Wales survey.' *Medical Journal of Australia 10*, 299–301.

Harrison, A., Long, K., Tommet, D. and Jones, R. (2017) 'Examining the role of race, ethnicity, and gender on social and behavioral ratings within the Autism Diagnostic Observation Schedule.' *Journal of Autism and Developmental Disabilities 47*, 2770–2782.

Harry, B. (1992) *Cultural Diversity, Families and Special Education System*. New York: Teachers College Press.

Harry, B. (2008) 'Collaboration with culturally and linguistically diverse families: Ideal versus reality.' *Exceptional Children 74*(3), 372–388.

Hatton, C., Akram, Y., Shah, R., Robertson, J. and Emerson, E. (2004) *Supporting South Asian Families with a Child with Severe Disabilities*. London: Jessica Kingsley Publishers.

Hatton, C., Azmi, S., Caine, A. and Emerson, E. (1998) 'Informal carers of adolescents and adults with learning disabilities from South Asian communities.' *British Journal of Social Work 28*, 821–837.

Higgins, B. (2009) *Good Practice in Supporting Adults with Autism: Guidance for Commissioners and Statutory Services*. London: The National Autistic Society.

Howlin, P. and Moss, P. (2012) 'Adults with autism spectrum disorder.' *The Canadian Journal of Psychiatry 57*(5), 275–283.

Huer, M. (2000) 'Examining perceptions of graphic symbols across cultures: Preliminary study of the impact of culture/ethnicity.' *Augmentative & Alternative Communication 16*(3), 180–185.

Irvine, J. (1978) '"Wolof magical thinking" culture and conservation revisited.' *Journal for Cross-Cultural Psychology 9*, 300–310.

Jack, R., Garrod, O., Yu, H., Caldara, R. and Schyns, P. (2012) 'Facial expressions of emotion are not culturally universal.' *Proceedings of the National Academy of Sciences 109*(19), 7241–7244.

Jamin, J.R. (1994) 'Language and Socialization of Child in African Families Living in France.' In P. Greenfield and R. Cocking (eds) *Cross-cultural Roots of Minority Child Development* (pp.147–166). Mahwah, NJ: Lawrence Erlbaum Associates.

Jarrold, C., Gilchrist, I.D. and Bender, A. (2005) 'Embedded figures detection in autism and typical development: Preliminary evidence of a double dissociation in relationships with visual search.' *Developmental Science 8*, 344–351.

Jegatheesan, B., Fowler, S. and Miller, P. (2010a) 'From symptom recognition to services: How South Asian Muslim immigrant families navigate autism.' *Disability & Society 25*(7), 797–811.

Jegatheesan, B., Miller, P. and Fowler, S. (2010b) 'Autism from a religious perspective: A study of parental beliefs in South Asian Muslim immigrant families.' *Focus on Autism and Other Developmental Disabilities 25*(2), 98–109.

Ji, L., Peng, K. and Nisbett, R. (2000) 'Culture, control and perception of relationships in the environment.' *Journal of Personality and Social Psychology 78*, 943–955.

Joe, J.R. (1994) 'Revaluing Native American Concepts of Development and Education.' In P. Greenfield and R. Cocking (eds) *Cross-cultural Roots of Minority Child Development* (pp.107–113). Mahwah, NJ: Lawrence Erlbaum Associates.

John Lian, M. (1996) 'Teaching Asian American Children.' In E. Duran (ed.) *Teaching Students with Moderate/Severe Disabilities, Including Autism* (2nd edn) (Chapter 11). Springfield, MO: Charles Thomas.

Kanner, L. (1943) 'Autistic disturbances of affective contact.' *Nervous Child 2*, 217–250.

Keen, D., Reid, F. and Arnone, D. (2010) 'Autism, ethnicity and maternal immigration.' *The British Journal of Psychiatry 196*, 274–281.

Kim, H.U. (2012) 'Autism across cultures: Rethinking autism.' *Disability & Society 27*(4), 535–545.

Kim, W., Kim, L. and Rue, D. (1997) 'Korean American Children.' In G. Johnson-Powell and J. Yamamoto (eds) *Transcultural Child Development – Psychological Assessment and Treatment* (pp.183–207). New York: John Wiley & Sons.

Kim, Y., Leventhal, B., Koh, Y., Fombonne, E., *et al.* (2011) 'Prevalence of ASD in Korean school-aged children.' *American Journal of Psychiatry 168*(9), 904–912.

Kitayama, S., Duffy, S., Kawamura, T. and Larsen, J. (2003) 'Perceiving an object and its context in different cultures: A cultural look at new look.' *Psychological Science 14*, 201–206.

Kleinman, A. (1986) 'Concepts and a Model of the Comparison of Medical Systems as Cultural Systems.' In C. Currer and M. Stacey (eds) *Concepts of Health, Illness and Disease: A Comparative Perspective* (pp.27–50). Leamington Spa: Berg.

Knapp, M., Hall, J. and Horgan, T. (2013) *Nonverbal Communication in Human Interaction*. Boston, MA: Wadsworth Cengage Learning.

Koh, H. and Milne, E. (2012) 'Evidence for a cultural influence on field-independence in autism spectrum disorder.' *Journal of Autism and Developmental Disorders 42*, 181–190.

Kolevzon, A., Gross, R. and Reichenberg, A. (2007) 'Prenatal and perinatal risk factors in autism.' *Archives of Paediatric and Adolescent Medicine 161*, 326–333.

LaFrance, M. and Mayo, C. (1976) 'Racial differences in gaze behavior during conversations: Two systematic observational studies.' *Journal of Personality and Social Psychology 33*(5), 547–552.

Lancy, D. (2007) 'Accounting for variability in mother–child play.' *American Anthropologist 109*(2), 273–284.

Lane, H. (1977) *The Wild Boy of Aveyron*. London: Allen & Unwin.

Lang, R., Rispoli, M., Sigafoos, J., Lancioni, G., Andrews, A. and Ortega, L. (2011) 'Effects of language of instruction on response accuracy and challenging behavior in a child with autism.' *Journal of Behavioral Education 20*, 252–259.

Lawson, J., Baron-Cohen, S. and Wheelwright, S. (2004) 'Empathising and systemising in adults with and without Asperger syndrome.' *Journal of Autism and Developmental Disorders 34*, 301–310.

Lee, H. (2011) 'Cultural factors related to the hidden curriculum for students with autism and related disabilities.' *Intervention in School and Clinic 46*(3), 141–149.

Leekam, S., Nieto, C., Libby, S., Wing, L. and Gould, J. (2007) 'Describing the sensory abnormalities of children and adults with autism.' *Journal of Autism and Developmental Disorders 37*, 894–910.

Levy, S., Mandell, D., Merhar, S., Ittenbach, R. and Pinto-Martin, J. (2003) 'Use of complementary and alternative medicine among children recently diagnosed with autistic spectrum disorder.' *Journal of Developmental and Behavioral Pediatrics 24*, 418–423.

Lindsay, G., Pather, S. and Strand, S. (2006) *Special Educational Needs and Ethnicity: Issues of Over- and Under-representation*. DfES Research Report 757. Nottingham: Department for Education and Skills.

Liptak, G., Benzoni, L., Mruzek, D., Nolan, K.W., *et al.* (2008) 'Disparities in diagnosis and access to health services for children with autism: Data from the National Survey of Children's Health.' *Journal of Developmental and Behavioral Pediatrics 29*, 152–160.

Liu, G. (2005) 'Best Practices – Developing Cross-cultural Competence from a Chinese Perspective.' In J. Stone (ed.) *Culture and Disability* (pp.65–86). Los Angeles, CA: Sage Publications.

Lord, C., Rutter, M., Di Lavore, P. and Risi, S. (1999) *Autism Diagnostic Observation Schedule.* Los Angeles, CA: Western Psychological Services.

Lotter, V. (1978) 'Childhood autism in Africa.' *Journal of Child Psychology and Psychiatry 19*, 231–244.

Magaña, S. and Smith, M. (2006) 'Psychological distress and well-being of Latina and non-Latina white mothers of youth and adults with an autism spectrum disorder: Cultural attitudes towards coresidence status.' *American Journal of Orthopsychiatry 76*(3), 346–357.

Magaña, S., Kristina, L., Aguinaga, A. and Morton, H. (2013) 'Access to diagnosis and treatment services among Latino children with autism spectrum disorders.' *Intellectual and Developmental Disabilities 51*(3), 141–153.

Mandell, D., Listerud, J., Levy, S. and Pinto-Martin, J. (2002) 'Race differences in the age at diagnosis among Medicaid-eligible children with autism.' *Journal of the American Academy of Child and Adolescent Psychiatry 41*, 1447–1453.

Mandell, D., Wiggins, L., Carpenter, L., Daniels, J., *et al.* (2009) 'Racial/ ethnic disparities in the identification of children with autism spectrum disorders.' *American Journal of Public Health 99*(3), 493–498.

Mansell, S., Sobsey, D. and Moskal, R. (1998) 'Clinical findings among sexually abused children with and without developmental disabilities.' *Mental Retardation 36*, 12–22.

Marchant, P., Hussain, A. and Hall, K. (2006) 'Autistic spectrum disorders and Asian children.' *British Journal of Education Studies 54*, 230–244.

Masuda, T. and Nisbett, R. (2006) 'Culture and change blindness.' *Cognitive Science 30*, 381–399.

Masuda, T., Ellsworth, P., Mesquita, B., Leu, J., *et al.* (2008) 'Placing the face in context: Cultural differences in the perception of facial emotion.' *Journal of Personality and Social Psychology 94*, 365–381.

Matson, J., Worley, J., Fodstad, J., Chung, K.M., *et al.* (2011) 'A multinational study examining the cross cultural differences in reported symptoms of autism spectrum disorders: Israel, South Korea, the United Kingdom, and the United States of America.' *Research in Autism Spectrum Disorders 5*, 1598–1604.

Matsumoto, D. (1994) *People – Psychology from a Cultural Perspective.* Pacific Grove, CA: Brooks & Cole.

Matsumoto, D. (2009) 'Culture and Emotional Expression.' In R. Wyer, C. Chiu and Y. Hong (eds) *Understanding Culture: Theory, Research, and Application* (pp.263–279). London: Psychology Press.

Maudsley, H. (1867) *The Physiology and Pathology of Mind.* New York: Appleton.

Mbise, A.S. and Kysela, G.M. (1990) 'Developing Appropriate Screening and Assessment Instruments: The Case of Tanzania.' In M.J. Thorburn and K. Marfo (eds) *Practical Approaches to Childhood Disability in Developing Countries: Insights from Experience and Research* (pp.225–243). St John's, Newfoundland, Canada: Memorial University of Newfoundland.

McCarthy, A., Lee, K., Itakura, S. and Muir, D.W. (2006) 'Cultural display rules drive eye gaze during thinking.' *Journal of Cross-Cultural Psychology 37*(6), 717–722.

McKone, E., Davies, A., Fernando, D., Aalders, R., *et al.* (2010) 'Asia has the global advantage: Race and visual attention.' *Vision Research 50*, 1540–1549.

Miller, D. (2005) 'An Introduction to Jamaican Culture for Rehabilitation Service Providers.' In J. Stone (ed.) *Culture and Disability* (pp.87–114). Thousand Oaks, CA: Sage Publications.

Mink, I.T. (1997) 'Studying culturally diverse families of children with mental retardation.' *International Review of Research in Mental Retardation 20*, 75–98.

Mirza, I., Tareen, A., Davidson, L.L. and Rahman, A. (2009) 'Community management of intellectual disabilities in Pakistan: A mixed methods study.' *Journal of Intellectual Disability Research 53*(6), 559–570.

Mouridsen, S., Rich, B., Torrben, R. and Nedergaard, N. (2008) 'Pervasive developmental disorder and criminal behaviour: A case controlled study.' *International Journal of Offender Therapy and Comparative Criminology 52*(2), 196–205.

Murphy, N. and Elias, E. (2006) 'Sexuality of children and adolescents with developmental disabilities.' *Pediatrics 118*, 398–403.

Nadig, A., Lee, I., Singh, L., Bosshart, K. and Ozonoff, S. (2010) 'How does the topic of conversation affect verbal exchange and eye gaze? A comparison between typical development and high-functioning autism.' *Neuropsychologia 48*, 2730–2739.

Nadirshaw, Z. (1998) 'Cultural Issues.' In J. O'Hara and A. Sperlinger (eds) *Adults with Learning Disabilities* (pp.139–153). Chichester: John Wiley & Sons.

Neal, L., McCray, A., Webb-Johnson, G. and Bridgest, S. (2003) 'The effects of African American movement styles on teachers' perceptions and reactions.' *The Journal of Special Education 37*, 49–57.

Nisbett, R. (2003) *The Geography of Thought: How Asians and Westerners Think Differently...and Why*. New York: The Free Press.

Norbury, C. and Sparks, A. (2013) 'Difference or disorder? Cultural issues in understanding neurodevelopmental disorders.' *Developmental Psychology 49*(1), 45–58.

Norbury, C., Brock, J., Cragg, L., Einav, S., Griffiths, H. and Nation, K. (2009) 'Eye-movement patterns are associated with communicative competence in autistic spectrum disorders.' *Journal of Child Psychology and Psychiatry 50*, 834–842.

Nsamenang, A.B. and Lamb, M.E. (1994) 'Socialization of Nso Children in the Bamenda Grass-fields of Northwest Cameroon.' In P. Greenfield and R. Cocking (eds) *Cross-cultural Roots of Minority Child Development* (pp.133–146). Mahwah, NJ: Lawrence Erlbaum Associates.

O'Hagan, K. (2001) *Cultural Competence in the Caring Professions*. London: Jessica Kingsley Publishers.

O'Toole, C. and Hickey, T.M. (2012) 'Diagnosing language impairment in bilinguals: Professional experience and perception.' *Child Language Teaching and Therapy 29*(1), 91–109.

Ogbu, J. (1994) 'From Cultural Differences to Differences in Cultural Frame of Reference.' In P. Greenfield and R. Cocking (eds) *Cross-cultural Roots of Minority Child Development* (pp.363–383). Mahwah, NJ: Lawrence Erlbaum Associates.

Owusu-Bempah, K. and Howitt, D. (2000) *Psychology beyond Western Perspectives*. Leicester: BPS Books.

Ozonoff, S. (1995) 'Executive Functions in Autism.' In E. Schopler and G.B. Mesibov (eds) *Learning and Cognition in Autism* (Chapter 11). New York: Plenum Press.

Pachter, L.M. and Dworkin, P.H. (1997) 'Maternal expectations about normal child development in 4 cultural groups.' *Archives of Paediatrics & Adolescent Medicine 151*, 1144–1150.

Park, H. (1996) 'Korean-American Families of Children with Disabilities: Perspectives and Implications for Practitioners.' In E. Duran (ed.) *Teaching Students with Moderate/Severe Disabilities, Including Autism* (2nd edn) (pp.194–214). Springfield, MO: Charles Thomas.

Pellicano, E., Gibson, L., Mayberry, M., Durkin, K. and Badcock, D. (2005) 'Abnormal global processing along the dorsal visual pathway in autism: A possible mechanism for weak visuospatial coherence?' *Neuropsychologia 43*, 1044–1053.

Perepa, P. (2007) 'Are ASD services for minority ethnic communities accessible?' *Good Autism Practice 8*(2), 3–8.

Perepa, P. (2009) 'Cultural Perceptions about Autism Spectrum Disorders and Social Behaviour: A Qualitative Study.' PhD thesis. University of Birmingham, UK.

Perepa, P. (2014) 'Cultural basis of social "deficits" in autism spectrum disorders.' *European Journal of Special Needs Education 29*(3), 313–326.

Petersen, J., Marinova-Todd, S. and Mirenda, P. (2012) 'Brief report: An exploratory study of lexical skills in bilingual children with autism spectrum disorders.' *Journal of Autism and Developmental Disorders 42*, 1499–1503.

Pierce, N., O'Reilly, M., Sorrells, A., Fragale, C., *et al.* (2014) 'Ethnicity reporting practices for empirical research in three autism related journals.' *Journal of Autism and Developmental Disorders 44*, 1507–1519.

Ratto, A., Reznick, S. and Turner-Brown, L. (2016) 'Cultural effects on the diagnosis of autism spectrum disorder among Latinos.' *Focus on Autism and Other Developmental Disabilities 31*(4), 275–283.

Ravindran, N. and Myers, B. (2012) 'Beliefs and practices regarding autism in Indian families now settled abroad: An internet survey.' *Focus on Autism and Other Developmental Disabilities 28*(1), 44–53.

Reichow, B., Volkmar, F. and Cicchetti, D. (2008) 'Development of the evaluative method for evaluating and determining evidence-based practices in autism.' *Journal of Autism and Developmental Disorders 38*, 1311–1319.

Reijneveld, S., Harland, P., Brugman, E., Verhulst, F. and Verloove-Vanhorick, S. (2005) 'Psychosocial problems among immigrant and non-immigrant children – Ethnicity plays a role in their occurrence and identification.' *European Child and Adolescent Psychiatry 14*, 145–152.

Robins, D., Fein, D. and Barton, M. (1999) *The Modified Checklist for Autism in Toddlers* (M-CHAT) [Self-published].

Rodriguez, B. and Olswang, L. (2003) 'Mexican-American and Anglo-American mothers' beliefs and values about child rearing, education, and language impairment.' *American Journal of Speech-Language Pathology 12*, 452–462.

Rogers-Adkinson, D., Ochoa, T. and Delgado, B. (2003) 'Developing cross-cultural competence: Serving families of children with significant developmental needs.' *Focus on Autism and Other Developmental Disabilities 18*(1), 4–8.

Romaine, S. (2008) 'Bilingual Language Development.' In M. Barrett (ed.) *The Development of Language* (Chapter 10). Hove: Psychology Press.

Roseberry-McKibbin, C. (2007) *Language Disorders in Children: A Multicultural and Case Perspective*. Boston, MA: Pearson Education.

Rutter, M. (1978) 'Diagnosis and definition of childhood autism.' *Journal of Autism and Childhood Schizophrenia 8*, 139–161.

Rutter, M., Bartak, L. and Newman, S. (1971) 'Autism – A Central Disorder of Cognition and Language?' In M. Rutter (ed.) *Infantile Autism: Concepts, Characteristics and Treatment* (pp.148–171). London: Churchill.

Rutter, M., Le Couteur, A. and Lord, C. (2005) *Autism Diagnostic Interview – Revised.* Los Angeles, CA: Western Psychological Services.

Salm, S.J. and Falola, T. (2002) *Culture and Customs of Ghana.* London: Greenwood Press.

Schieve, L., Boulet, S., Blumberg, S., Kogan, M., *et al.* (2012) 'Association between parental nativity and autism spectrum disorder among US-born non-Hispanic white and Hispanic children, 2007 National Survey of Children's Health.' *Disability and Health Journal 5*, 18–25.

Schofield, T.J., Parke, R.D., Kim, Y. and Coltrane, S. (2008) 'Bridging the acculturation gap: Parent–child relationship quality as a moderator in Mexican American families.' *Developmental Psychology 44*(4), 1190–1194.

Schopler, E. and van Bourgondien, M. (2010) *Childhood Autism Rating Scale* (2nd edn). Los Angeles, CA: Western Psychological Services.

Schulze, P., Harwood, R.L., Schoelmerich, A. and Leyendecker, B. (2002) 'The cultural structuring of parenting and universal developmental tasks.' *Parenting: Science and Practice 2*, 151–178.

Sell, N., Giarelli, E., Blum, N., Hanlon, A. and Levy, S. (2012) 'A comparison of autism spectrum disorder DSM-IV criteria and associated features among African American and white children in Philadelphia County.' *Disability and Health Journal 5*(1), 9–17.

Serwatka, T., Deering, S. and Grants, P. (1995) 'Disproportionate representation of African Americans in emotionally handicapped classes.' *Journal of Black Studies 25*, 492–506.

Seung, H., Siddiqi, S. and Elder, J. (2006) 'Intervention outcomes of a bilingual child with autism.' *Journal of Medical Speech-Language Pathology 14*(1), 53–63.

Shah, A. and Frith, U. (1983) 'An islet of ability in autistic children: A research note.' *Journal of Child Psychology and Psychiatry 24*, 613–620.

Shah, R. (1995) *The Silent Minority: Children with Disabilities in Asian Families* (2nd edn). London: National Children's Bureau.

Shaked, M. (2005) 'The social trajectory of illness: Autism in the ultraorthodox community in Israel.' *Social Science and Medicine 61*, 2190–2200.

Shin, Y., Lee, K., Min, S. and Emde, R. (1999) 'A Korean syndrome of attachment disturbance mimicking symptoms of pervasive developmental disorder.' *Infant Mental Health Journal 20*(1), 60–76.

Siponmaa, L., Kristiansson, M., Jonson, C., Nyden, A. and Gillberg, C. (2001) 'Juvenile and young adult mentally disordered offenders: The role of child neuropsychiatric disorders.' *Journal of the American Academy of Psychiatry Law 154*(2), 185–190.

Skahan, S., Watson, M. and Lof, G. (2007) 'Speech-language pathologists' assessment practices for children with suspected speech sound disorders: Results of a national survey.' *American Journal of Speech Language Pathology 16*(3), 246–259.

Skinner, D., Bailey, D., Correa, V. and Rodriguez, P. (1999) 'Narrating self and disability: Latino mothers' construction of identities vis-à-vis their child with special needs.' *Exceptional Children 65*, 481–495.

Skinner, D., Correa, V., Skinner, M. and Bailey, D. (2001) 'Role of religion in the lives of Latino families of young children with developmental delays.' *American Journal on Mental Retardation 106*, 297–313.

Sotgiu, I., Galati, D., Manzano, M., Gandione, M., *et al.* (2011) 'Parental attitudes, attachment styles, social networks, and psychological processes in autism spectrum disorders: A cross-cultural perspective.' *The Journal of Genetic Psychology: Research and Theory on Human Development 172*(4), 353–375.

Tait, K. and Mundia, L. (2012) 'The impact of a child with autism on the Bruneian family system.' *International Journal of Special Education 27*(3), 199–212.

Tharp, R.G. (1994) 'Intergroup Differences among Native Americans in Socialization and Child Cognition: An Ethnographic Analysis.' In P. Greenfield and R. Cocking (eds) *Cross-cultural Roots of Minority Child Development* (pp.87–105). Mahwah, NJ: Lawrence Erlbaum Associates.

Themba, C. and Lord, C. (2012) 'Longitudinal study of perceived negative impact in African American and Caucasian mothers of children with autism spectrum disorder.' *Autism 17*(4), 405–417.

Thomas, K., Ellis, A., McLaurin, C., Daniels, J. and Morrissey, J. (2007) 'Access to care for autism-related services.' *Journal of Autism and Developmental Disorders 37*(10), 1902–1913.

Tomblin, J. (2006) 'A normativist account of language-based learning disability.' *Learning Disabilities Research and Practice 21*, 8–18.

Trotter, R. and Chavira, J. (1997) *Curanderismo: Mexican-American Folk Healing.* Athens, GA: University of Georgia Press.

van Krevelen, D. (1971) 'Early infantile autism and autistic psychopathy.' *Journal of Autism and Childhood Schizophrenia 1*, 82–86.

Vrana, S. and Rollock, D. (2002) 'The role of ethnicity, gender, emotional content, and contextual differences in physiological, expressive, and self-reported emotional responses to imagery.' *Cognition and Emotion 16*(1), 165–192.

Wan, Y., Hu, Q., Li, T., Jiang, L., *et al.* (2013) 'Prevalence of autism spectrum disorders among children in China: A systematic review.' *Shanghai Archives of Psychiatry 25*, 70–80. doi: 10.3969/j.issn.1002-0829.2013.02.003

Webb, E. (2000) 'Health care for ethnic minorities.' *Current Paediatrics 10*, 184–190.

West, E., Travers, J., Kemper, T., Liberty, L., *et al.* (2016) 'Racial and ethnic diversity of participants in research supporting evidence-based practices for learners with autism spectrum disorder.' *The Journal of Special Education 50*(3), 151–163.

WHO (World Health Organization) (1993) *The ICD-10 Classification of Mental and Behavioural Disorders: Diagnostic Criteria for Research.* Geneva: WHO.

Wilder, L., Dyches, T., Obiakor, F. and Algozzine, B. (2004) 'Multicultural perspectives on teaching students with autism.' *Focus on Autism and Other Developmental Disabilities 19*(2), 105–113.

Williams, K., Helmer, M., Duncan, G., Peat, J. and Mellis, C. (2008) 'Perinatal and maternal risk factors for autism spectrum disorders in New South Wales, Australia.' *Child Care Health Development 34*, 249–256.

Wing, L. (1980) 'Childhood autism and social class: A question of selection?' *British Journal of Psychiatry 137*, 410–417.

Wing, L. and Gould, J. (1979) 'Severe impairments of social interaction and associated abnormalities in children: Epidemiology and classification.' *Journal of Autism and Childhood Schizophrenia 9*, 11–29.

Winter, K. (2001) 'Numbers of bilingual children in speech and language therapy: Theory and practice of measuring their representation.' *The International Journal of Bilingualism 5*(4), 465–495.

Wiredu, K. (1996) *Cultural Universals and Particulars – An African Perspective.* Bloomington, IN: Indiana University Press.

Wong, C., Odom, S., Hume, K., Cox, A., *et al.* (2014) *Evidence-based Practices for Children, Youth, and Young Adults with Autism Spectrum Disorder.* Chapel Hill, NC: The University of North Carolina, Frank Porter Graham, Child Development Institute, Autism Evidence-based Practice Review Group.

Woodbury-Smith, M., Clare, I., Holland, A. and Kearns, J. (2006) 'High functioning autistic spectrum disorders, offending and other law-breaking: Findings from a community sample.' *Journal of Forensic Psychiatry and Psychology 17*, 108–120.

Yuki, M., Maddux, W. and Masuda, T. (2007) 'Are the windows to the soul the same in the East and West? Cultural differences in using the eyes and mouth as cues to recognize emotions in Japan and the United States.' *Journal of Experimental Social Psychology 43*(2), 303–311.

Zhang, J., Wheeler, J. and Richey, D. (2006) 'Cultural validity in assessment instruments for children with autism from a Chinese cultural perspective.' *International Journal of Special Education 21*, 109–113.

Subject Index

Author Index